END

ENDS IN SIGHT

Marx/Fukuyama/Hobsbawm/Anderson

Gregory Elliott

Pluto Press
LONDON • ANN ARBOR, MI

and
Between the Lines
TORONTO

First published 2008 by Pluto Press
345 Archway Road, London N6 5AA
and 839 Greene Street, Ann Arbor, MI 48106
www.plutobooks.com

First published in Canada in 2008 by
Between the Lines
720 Bathurst Street, Suite #404
Toronto, Ontario   M5S 2R4
Canada
1-800-718-7201
www.btlbooks.com

British Library Cataloguing in Publication Data
A catalogue record for this book is available from the British Library

ISBN   978 0 7453 2763 1 (hardback)
ISBN   978 0 7453 2762 4 (Pluto paperback)
ISBN   978 1 8970 7140 3 (Between the Lines paperback)

Library of Congress Cataloging in Publication Data applied for

Library and Archives Canada Cataloguing in Publication
Elliott, Gregory
    Ends in sight : Marx/ Fukuyama/ Hobsbawn/ Anderson / Gregory
Elliott.
Includes bibliographical references and index.
ISBN 978-1-897071-40-3
    1. Marx, Karl, 1818-1883. Manifest der Kommunistischen Partei.
2. Socialism. 3. Capitalism. 4. Fukuyama, Francis. 5. Hobsbawm, E. J.
(Eric J.), 1917-. 6. Anderson, Perry. I. Title.
HX73.E423 2008   335.4   C2007-906315-2

This book is printed on paper suitable for recycling and made from
fully managed and sustained forest sources. Logging, pulping and
manufacturing processes are expected to conform to the environmental
regulations of the country of origin.

10   9   8   7   6   5   4   3   2   1

Designed and produced for Pluto Press by
Chase Publishing Services Ltd, Fortescue, Sidmouth EX10 9QG
Typeset from disk by Stanford DTP Services, Northampton
Printed and bound in the United States of America

*In memory of Christopher Hill, past master;
and of Joe McCarney, old friend*

Contents

Preface

The final decades of the twentieth century witnessed numerous sightings of a certain 'end of history' or the end of a certain history; and – if only implicitly – the inception of another. (To sense an ending is invariably to scent a beginning.) Among them, at least three retain significance for the left, by virtue of the intrinsic interest of their subject matter (the past results and future prospects of capitalism and socialism), the force of their provocation and the breadth of their perspective. Moreover, Francis Fukuyama, Eric Hobsbawm and Perry Anderson all in some measure took their bearings, if only to plot a contrary course, from Marx, the 150th anniversary of whose most widely diffused text in 1998 found him lauded as seer of capitalist 'globalisation'.

Ends in Sight appraises these historical panoramas, offered from opposing standpoints (one neo-conservative, three variously socialist) and on contrasting scales (political manifesto, philosophy of history, account of the twentieth century, inaugural editorial). Relating them to other writings by their authors, each chapter may stand as a separate composition. But they are scored here as an unwitting quartet.

Taking the *Communist Manifesto* as a founding document of historical materialism, Chapter 1 focuses on Marx's projection of an end of human 'pre-history' in communism, delineating his differentiation of 'scientific' from 'utopian' socialism and distilling the verdicts of his descendants, from Labriola on the eve of the twentieth century down to Hobsbawm at its close. The second chapter re-examines Fukuyama's *The End of History and the Last Man* (1992), following his defection from the intellectual camp most closely associated in public opinion with imperialist war in Iraq, and his subsequent efforts (e.g. in the Afterword to a new edition of the book) to edulcorate the original message derived from his inversion of Marx's 'materialist conception of history'. Hobsbawm's dismissive reaction to Fukuyama leads, in Chapter 3, into a discussion of *Age of Extremes* (1994) and subsequent supplementations of it, most recently in *Globalisation, Democracy and Terrorism*. Notwithstanding an oblique vindication of the role of communism, the conclusion of the 'short twentieth century' as depicted by Hobsbawm is argued to have more in common with various antagonists (including Fukuyama) than its author realises. In Chapter 4, a brief but significant statement – 'Renewals' (2000) – by a figure who has commented at length on Fukuyama and Hobsbawm is subjected to scrutiny. Resistance to the underlying trend of the times, combined with a determination accurately to reflect it, is identified as the source of Perry Anderson's reticence about the 'alter-globalisation' movement. Finally, returning to a topic touched on in Chapter 1, a short Conclusion seeks to take the temperature of the anti-capitalist wing of that 'movement of movements', which would vindicate Marx and contradict Fukuyama, Hobsbawm and Anderson.

Written from the disadvantage point of an intransigent left, this opuscule is nevertheless unlikely to go down well with sections of it, old and new. This is perhaps especially true of the Conclusion, which, in tying together some of the threads of the arguments advanced in the first four chapters, states 'conclusions without premises' on various of the wider issues raised. Necessarily schematic, even dogmatic, it largely upholds the sense of an ending articulated, in their different ways, by Hobsbawm and Anderson; and therewith ratifies the sense of a beginning implicit in it – that is, of a historical epoch in which, for the first time in more than a century and a half, capitalism has not been haunted by its shadow: the spectre of socialism. This in no way grants eternal life to the complacent, globally unbound Prometheus of the new millennium (after all, as Hobsbawm maintains, capitalism may be in the process of devouring itself). Nor does it entail the enduring triumph of its US variant – only one of the possibilities envisioned by Fukuyama. But it does imply the implausibility, in any *foreseeable* future, of the kind of systemic alternative to capitalism long represented by what, following Norberto Bobbio, must now be referred to as historical socialism.

Before proceeding, as someone who still calls himself a Marxist depending on who's asking, I am bound to add a word or two on the subject. For now, I shall do so in the words of another – Maurice Merleau-Ponty, in the Preface to *Signs* (1960), registering the misadventures of the dialectic: 'Marxism has definitely entered a new phase of its history, in which it can inspire and orient analyses and retain a certain heuristic value, but is certainly no longer true *in the sense it was believed to be true*.'[1] To which I would only add the Latin tag employed by Domenico Losurdo, in the Introduction to an Italian edition of the *Communist Manifesto*, to encapsulate his relationship to Marx: *Nec tecum possum vivere nec sine te!* (can't live with or without you!).[2]

Acknowledgements

The chapters below appear here for the first time, although I have occasionally drawn upon related publications. Chapter 1 is a greatly expanded version of a talk given at the University of Brighton in 2002. Chapter 2 uses some passages from a previous article dealing with Fukuyama, 'The Cards of Confusion: Reflections on Historical Communism and the "End of History"' (*Radical Philosophy*, no. 64, Summer 1993), as well as from 'Velocities of Change: Perry Anderson's Sense of an Ending' (*Historical Materialism*, no. 2, Summer 1998). Chapter 3 has its distant origins in a seminar paper at Sussex University in 1995, but has been radically recast and updated. Chapter 4 contains material from the Postscript to the Spanish edition of my *Perry Anderson: The Merciless Laboratory of History* (University of Valencia Press, 2004) and a reworked introductory paragraph from 'Velocities of Change'. The Conclusion incorporates a few pages from the Brighton talk referred to above.

Thanks are owed to Anne Beech, the staff of Pluto Press and its anonymous referees for commission, production and publication; to Justin Rosenberg, Warren Montag and Tom Hickey for help along the way; and to Lekha and Emmanuel on the one hand, Ian Horobin on the other, for their respective grants of living and work space.

ONE

The Sorcerer and the Gravedigger: Karl Marx

'The return of Marx': thus the *New Yorker* of all places, as the 150th anniversary of the *Communist Manifesto* approached, hailing its main author as prophet of a globalised capitalism and its distempers.[1] Seemingly dispelled, along with the 'spectre of communism' he had conjured up in the exordium to the *Manifesto*, the revenant had something to impart less than a decade after the collapse of states forged in his name. By 2005, he could comfortably win a contest staged by a BBC radio programme to choose the 'greatest philosopher', prompting a two-page anathema in the *Daily Mail* against 'Marx the Monster' that laid direct responsibility for no fewer than 150 million corpses at his door.[2]

For less overwrought commentators, wherein consisted the 'actuality' of Marx's thought as epitomised by the *Communist Manifesto*? According to Eric Hobsbawm, introducing a re-edition of the text in 1998, it provided 'a concise characterization of capitalism at the end of the twentieth century'

– a judgement seconded by Gareth Stedman Jones, for whom the *Manifesto* offered a 'brief but still quite unsurpassed depiction of modern capitalism'.[3] Uniquely prescient as regards capitalism, a certain consensus might be summarised, Marx had been singularly mistaken about communism. But if the former, how come the latter? For the one message that unmistakably emerges from the text is this: communism is inherent in capitalism. Consequently, to vindicate the contemporaneity of the *Communist Manifesto* by recasting it as a non-manifesto without the communism might be reckoned a prime example of praising with damn, faint or fulsome as you will.

CONTRARIES

At all events, no such plaudits had been forthcoming from any quarter when the 23-page *Manifesto of the Communist Party* was originally published in German in London, on the eve of the 1848 revolutions. While it scarcely fell dead-born from the press à la Hume, it was unquestionably a premature birth. Over the next half-century, however, it achieved canonical status in the working-class labour and socialist parties of the developed world. Anticipating its fiftieth anniversary, the leading Italian Marxist philosopher Antonio Labriola opened his famous 1896 essay 'In Memoria del Manifesto dei comunisti' as follows:

All those in our ranks who have a desire or an occasion to possess a better understanding of their own work should bring to mind the causes and moving forces which determined the genesis of the Manifesto. ... Only in this way will it be possible for us to find in the present social form the explanation of the tendency towards socialism, thus showing by its present necessity the inevitability of its triumph.

Is not that in fact the vital part of the Manifesto, its essence and its distinctive character?[4]

A résumé of Marx and Engels's 'materialist conception of history', the *Manifesto* marked the 'passage from utopia to science'.[5]

As a privileged correspondent of Engels, Labriola enjoyed a prestigious warrant for such claims. In 1880 Engels had issued *Socialism: Utopian and Scientific* – a pamphlet extracted from *Anti-Dühring* (1878), in which he systematised the dialectical and historical materialism of the 'communist world outlook championed by Marx and myself',[6] thereby marking another fateful passage: the transition from Marx to Marxism, in the first of its authorised versions. 'The socialism of earlier days', Engels argued,

certainly criticised the existing capitalistic mode of production and its consequences. But it could not explain them, and, therefore, could not get the mastery of them. It could only simply reject them as bad. The more strongly this earlier socialism

denounced the exploitation of the working class
... the less able was it clearly to show in what this
exploitation consisted and how it arose. But for
this it was necessary – (1) to present the capitalistic
method of production in its historical connection
and its inevitableness during a particular historical
period, and therefore, also, to present its inevitable
downfall; and (2) to lay bare its essential character,
which was still a secret. This was done by the
discovery of *surplus value*. ...

These two great discoveries, the materialistic
conception of history and the revelation of the
secret of capitalistic production through surplus
value, we owe to Marx. With these discoveries
socialism became a science.[7]

Described by Labriola as an 'obituary notice' on the
bourgeoisie and its mode of production, the *Communist
Manifesto* was indivisibly the announcement of a
birth: communism.

A later distinguished Italian historian of Marxist
thought adjudged Engels's pamphlet 'not so much the
best interpretation of [it] as *the* interpretation of it'.[8] In
one respect, this cannot be altogether accurate, since
the second of the 'great discoveries' it attributes to
Marx – the theory of surplus value, with its decisive
differentiation between labour and labour power – had
not been made by 1848 and was only fully elaborated
in Volume 1 of *Capital* some twenty years later. The
Manifesto's account of capitalist exploitation is that of
a Ricardian – not a Marxian – communist, involving

a subsistence theory of wages. On the other hand, the materialist conception of history had, in its essentials, been formulated in the mid 1840s, in *The German Ideology*. Thus, Marx's general theory of history, if not his special theory of capitalist society, did indeed underpin the depiction of historical trajectory contained in the *Manifesto* – something Marx himself effectively registered by opting to quote a key passage from it, on the 'fall [of the bourgeoisie] and the victory of the proletariat', in a closing footnote to Chapter 32 of *Capital* Volume 1 ('The Historical Tendency of Capitalist Accumulation').[9] Moreover, in their joint Preface to the German Edition of 1872, Marx and Engels, sounding a leitmotif of Marxist commentary on the *Manifesto*, insisted that '[h]owever much the state of things may have altered during the last twenty-five years, the general principles laid down in the Manifesto are, on the whole, as correct today as ever'.[10] Sixteen years later, prefacing an English edition, Engels cited this statement immediately after his précis of the 'fundamental proposition' – the materialist conception of history – that provided the *Manifesto* with its 'nucleus'.[11]

What was that 'fundamental proposition', 'destined [so Engels ventured] to do for history what Darwin's theory has done for biology'?[12] Its most compact statement is to be found in the 1859 Preface to *A Contribution to the Critique of Political Economy*. Introduced as the 'general conclusion' Marx had arrived at c. 1845, it comprises:

1. a morphology of social structure as a combination of economic infrastructure (forces plus relations of productions) and a 'corresponding' superstructure (juridico-political institutions and 'forms of social consciousness'), in which the economic has explanatory primacy;

2. an account of the overall trajectory of human history, construing it as a succession of 'progressive' economic modes of production – Asiatic, ancient, feudal, capitalist – and the social formations rooted in them, terminating in communism;

3. a theory of 'epochal' social change, identifying the intermittent non-correspondence (contradiction) between the forces and relations of production as the principal mechanism of the transition from one mode of production to another.

On this account, the relations of production constitute the economic structure of society – the distribution of the means of production to economic agents and the consequent distribution of those agents to antagonistic social classes – and condition the superstructure. They are transformed when they impede, rather than facilitate, the development of the productive forces. The 'era of social revolution' set in train by such 'fettering' ends with the installation of superior relations of production, now adequate to the productive forces; and the transformation of the superstructure, now duly equipped to secure the infrastructure. In this dialectic of the forces (content) and relations (form) of production, the growth of the former characterises the general course of history and ultimately explains it. Capitalism is the last 'antagonistic' socio-economic formation, because its productive forces 'create ... the material conditions for a solution of this antagonism' – a supersession of capitalism by communism that will close the 'pre-history of human society'.[13]

This is a 'materialist' philosophy of history in which history is directional, not cyclical; and progressive, not regressive. At the same time, however, the pattern of the progress it divines is not so much rectilinear as 'dialectical'. As a result, history can progress by the 'bad side' – indeed, for the most part it has. In the properly Marxian perspective on capitalism, it is (in Fredric Jameson's fine phrase) 'at one and the same time the best thing that has ever happened to the human race, and the worst'.[14] The grounds for such an assessment were incomparably laid out by Marx in a speech made in 1856:

> On the one hand, there have started into life industrial and scientific forces which no epoch of ... former human history had ever suspected. On the other hand, there exist symptoms of decay, far surpassing the horrors recorded of the latter times of the Roman empire. In our days everything seems pregnant with its contrary. Machinery, gifted with the wonderful power of shortening and fructifying human labour, we behold starving and overworking it. The new-fangled sources of wealth, by some strange weird spell, are turned into sources of want. The victories

of art seem bought by the loss of character. At the same time that mankind masters nature, man seems to become enslaved to other men or to his own infamy. Even the pure light of science seems unable to shine but on the dark background of ignorance. All our invention and progress seem to result in endowing material forces with intellectual life, and in stultifying human life into a material force. This antagonism between modern industry and science on the one hand, modern misery and dissolution on the other hand; this antagonism between the productive powers, and the social relations of our epoch is a fact, palpable, overwhelming, and not to be controverted.[15]

Any unilateral estimate, whether negative or positive, betrays the contradictoriness of capitalism as a historical phenomenon. To perceive only its negative aspects is to lapse into romanticism, hankering after an allegedly better past; to be oblivious of them is to indulge in the utilitarianism of the 'bourgeois viewpoint', transfiguring a supposedly untranscendable present.[16] As Marshall Berman's celebrated reading of the dialectic of modernity in the *Manifesto* demonstrates,[17] what Marx seeks to do is overcome any such antithesis intellectually, while pointing to its transcendence practically. It contains an appreciation of the sense in which capitalism at once creates and frustrates the emancipatory promise of modernity, whose full potential can only be released and realised in the future by revolution, in the specifi-cally modern sense of comprehensive political and social transformation. Thus, in Marx's emphatic declaration in the *Manifesto*, '[i]n bourgeois society ... the past dominates the present; in communist society, the present dominates the past'.[18] *Du passé faisons table rase!*, as the *Internationale* has it. Communism is indeed the wave of the future. Humanity 'only sets itself such tasks as it can solve';[19] and communism – a clean sweep of the past – is the solution to what, in the 1844 *Economic and Philosophical Manuscripts*, Marx called the 'riddle of history'.[20]

CHRONICLE OF A DEATH – AND A BIRTH – FORETOLD

For our purposes, we may largely set to one side both section III of the *Manifesto*, where Marx demarcates his own text from previous 'socialist and communist literature', reproved in its generality for a 'total incapacity to comprehend the march of modern history';[21] and the cursory fourth and final section devoted to the 'position of the communists in relation to the various existing opposition parties'. Instead, we shall be concerned with the 'theoretical conclusions of the Communists' adumbrated in the core of the *Manifesto* – i.e. the first two sections on 'bourgeois and proletarians' and 'proletarians and communists' – of which (echoing a passage in *The German Ideology*) it is asserted that they 'are in no way based on ideal principles that have been invented, or discovered, by this or that would-be universal reformer. They merely express, in general terms, actual relations springing from an existing class struggle, from a historical movement going on under our very eyes.'[22]

Those conclusions might be encapsulated thus: capitalism, highest form of class society, generates the necessary and sufficient conditions, material and social, for a classless society. In a word, capitalism creates communism. How so? The short answer is: on account of the intrinsically contradictory, and finally self-destructive, dynamics of its own development. Hence section I is given over to what Labriola dubbed a 'funeral oration' for the bourgeoisie, adding: 'Never was funeral oration so magnificent.'[23] Itself 'the product of a long course of development, of a series of revolutions in the modes of production and exchange',[24] the bourgeoisie, Marx averred, 'historically, has played a most revolutionary part', portrayed by him in epic terms that defy paraphrase:

> ... wherever it has got the upper hand, [it] has put an end to all feudal, patriarchal, idyllic relations ... and has left remaining no other nexus between man and man than naked self-interest, than callous 'cash payment'. ... It has resolved personal worth into exchange value, and ... set up that single unconscionable freedom – free trade. In one word, for exploitation, veiled by religious and political illusions, it has substituted naked, shameless, direct, brutal exploitation. ... It has been the first to show what man's activity can bring about. It

has accomplished wonders far surpassing Egyptian pyramids, Roman aqueducts, and Gothic cathedrals; it has conducted expeditions that put in the shade all former exoduses of nations and crusades. The bourgeoisie cannot exist without constantly revolutionizing the instruments of production, and thereby the relations of production, and with them the whole relation of society. ... Constant revolutionizing of production, uninterrupted disturbance of all social conditions, everlasting uncertainty and agitation distinguish the bourgeois epoch from all earlier ones. All fixed, fast-frozen relations, with their train of ancient and venerable prejudices and opinions, are swept away, all new-formed ones become antiquated before they can ossify. All that is solid melts into air, all that is holy is profaned. ... The need of a constantly expanding market for its products chases the bourgeoisie over the surface of the globe. It must nestle everywhere, settle everywhere, establish connections everywhere. The bourgeoisie has through its exploitation of the world market given a cosmopolitan character to production and consumption in every country. ... In place of the old local and national seclusion and self-sufficiency, we have intercourse in every direction, universal interdependence of nations. The bourgeoisie, by the rapid development of all instruments of production, by the immensely facilitated means of communication, draws all ... nations into civilization. The cheap prices of its commodities are the heavy artillery with which it batters down all Chinese walls.... It forces all nations ... to adopt the bourgeois mode of production; it compels them to introduce what it calls civilization into their midst, i.e., to become bourgeois themselves. In one word, it creates a world after its own image. ... The bourgeoisie, during its rule of scarce one hundred years, has created more massive and more colossal productive forces than have all preceding generations put together.[25]

Capitalism is here reduced to the bourgeoisie (or elided with it).[26] As in the 1859 Preface, it is not named as such in the text, where it is referred to by the concept of 'bourgeois mode of production' and 'bourgeois society'. Be that as it may, the unsustainable hypertrophy of global capitalist expansion contains the seeds of its own destruction. For just as feudal relations of production came to 'fetter' the development of the productive forces, and were eventually sundered by the 'rising bourgeoisie',[27] so:

A similar movement is going on before our own eyes. Modern bourgeois society ... is like the sorcerer, who is no longer able to control the powers of the nether world whom he has called up by his spells. For many a decade past, the history of industry and commerce is but the history of the revolt of the modern productive forces against modern conditions of production, against the property relations that are the conditions for the existence of the bourgeoisie and its rule.[28]

The contradiction between expanding, socialised productive forces and constricting private property relations finds expression in endemic 'commercial crises'. Resolution of them by recourse to the exploitation of new markets, or more intensive exploitation of old ones, is self-defeating in the long run, serving as it does only to 'pav[e] the way for more extensive and destructive crises, by diminishing the means whereby crises are prevented'.[29] Accordingly, if, for all its depredations, capitalism is to be lauded for having played a progressive role historically, by developing the productive forces on a world scale, Marx's diagnosis of its present modus operandi is unequivocal – irrationality and inhumanity – and his prognosis similarly stark: suicide – or rather, euthanasia administered by the proletariat.

The anarchy of capitalist production has generated the material prerequisites for it to be supplanted: abolition of the 'realm of necessity', rooted in scarcity. Crucially, it has also created the requisite social conditions for attaining the 'realm of freedom': the emergence of a collective agent, in the shape of the organised, class-conscious industrial proletariat, with both a material interest in 'entirely revolutionizing the mode of production'[30] and the indispensable structural capacity so to do. Far from being implacable, the capitalist social structure is by turns constraining and enabling of human agency. Indeed, at a certain stage of its development – manifestly thought impending by Marx – the balance between constraint and empowerment shifts, and capitalist social structure enables the collective agency of the proletariat to arrest the largely involuntary process of capitalist reproduction and initiate the process of its conscious communist transformation, thereby (re)making history. The second of the *Manifesto*'s dramatis personae, the proletariat, 'alone is a really revolutionary class'.[31] It is to capitalism as the bourgeoisie was to feudalism:

> The weapons with which the bourgeoisie felled feudalism to the ground are now turned against the bourgeoisie itself. But not only has the bourgeoisie forged the weapons that bring death to itself; it has also called into existence the men who are to wield those weapons – the modern working class – the proletarians.[32]

The modern working class, 'essential and special product' of capitalist industry,[33] has an overwhelming material interest in the abolition of the capitalist mode of production for a very simple reason. When it comes to distribution of its fruits between the direct producers whose labour produces them and the owners of the means of production who appropriate them, capitalism is in effect a zero-sum game:

> The modern labourer, ... instead of rising with the progress of industry, sinks deeper and deeper below the conditions of existence of his class. He becomes a pauper, and pauperism develops more rapidly than population and wealth. And here it becomes evident that the bourgeoisie is unfit any longer to be the ruling class in society, and to impose its conditions of existence upon society as

an overriding law. It is unfit to rule because it is incompetent to assure an existence to its slave within his slavery, because it cannot help letting him sink into such a state that it has to feed him, instead of being fed by him. Society can no longer live under this bourgeoisie, in other words, its existence is no longer compatible with society.[34]

In the *Manifesto*, proletarian pauperisation – the tendency for ever more workers to become dependent upon public provision – indicates a trend to their absolute immiseration in capitalist society, as real wages tend to decline. In *Capital*, by contrast, once Marx had worked out his mature economic theory, two tendencies are distinguished: periodic *absolute* impoverishment of sections of the working class through unemployment; and *relative* impoverishment of the whole working class by dint of increased exploitation on the one hand and the non-satisfaction of historically developed human needs on the other – and these regardless of any rise in real wages. Hence although the precise details altered significantly, the postulate of an objective proletarian material interest in the abolition of capitalism did not.

An anti-capitalist material interest on the part of the proletariat does not in and of itself guarantee a commensurate anti-capitalist – or, a fortiori, pro-communist – class capacity. Ascription of the latter is likewise rooted in what the leading theorist of the Second International, Karl Kautsky, identified as 'the suicidal tendencies of the capitalist system':[35] the simplification of class structure and polarisation of class antagonisms, ranging 'two great hostile camps'[36] against one another; the proleterianisation of the 'lower strata of the middle class' and a corresponding augmentation of working-class numbers; the inexorable concentration and combination of the proletariat, issuing in 'the ever-expanding union of the workers', their 'organization ... into a class, and consequently into a political party'.[37] And that 'party' has two intimately connected defining characteristics. First, unlike '[a]ll previous historical movements', it is 'the self-conscious, independent movement of the immense majority, in the interest of the immense majority'.[38] Second, again in contrast to movements of the exploited and oppressed under prior modes of production, the 'proletarians cannot become masters of the productive forces of society, except by abolishing ... every other previous mode of appropriation':

> The distinguishing feature of Communism is ... the abolition of bourgeois property. But modern bourgeois private property is the final and most complete expression of the system of producing and appropriating products, that is based on class antagonisms, on the exploitation of the many by the few.[39]

To mix Marx's metaphors, then, the sorcerer inadvertently summons up his gravedigger:

> The advance of industry ... replaces the isolation
> of the labourers, due to competition, by their
> revolutionary combination, due to association.
> The development of Modern Industry, therefore,
> cuts from under its feet the very foundation on
> which the bourgeoisie produces and appropriates
> products. What the bourgeoisie, therefore, produces,
> above all, is its own grave-diggers. Its fall and the
> victory of the proletariat are equally inevitable.[40]

At the outset, when predicating of all (recorded)
human history that it had been a history of class
struggles, Marx did of course observe that this was
'a fight that each time ended, either in a revolutionary
reconstitution of society at large, or in the common ruin
of the contending classes'.[41] He therewith introduced
a distinction, and opened up a gap, between the
'inevitable fall' of the bourgeoisie on the one hand
and the 'inevitable victory' of the proletariat on the
other. Still, the stress in the remainder of the text, and
throughout the subsequent career of orthodox Marxism,
incontrovertibly fell on the conjoint character of these
outcomes. The 'historical mission' of the proletariat
(adverted to by Engels in the closing lines of *Socialism:
Utopian and Scientific*)[42] was to emancipate itself and,
in so doing, to liberate the whole of humanity from
the exploitation and oppression of capitalism, latest
and last instantiation of class society. The immanent
– and imminent – future of capitalism, the only feasible,
viable and desirable one, was communism. Communist
revolution was, as it were, inscribed in the genetic

code of capitalist evolution. Not only the abolition of capitalism, but also its replacement by communism, was necessary and inevitable. The requisite material and social conditions for 'entirely revolutionizing the mode of production'[43] also happened to be sufficient. History proposes; the proletariat disposes.

Communists of the Marxian variety were thus said to have 'over the great mass of the proletariat the advantage of clearly understanding the line of march, the conditions, and the ultimate general result of the proletarian movement'.[44] They were immeasurably aided in this by the rallying to the communist cause of 'bourgeois ideologists, who have raised themselves to the level of comprehending theoretically the historical movement as a whole'. But it is the 'historical movement as a whole',[45] not a political party (in pre-modern or modern senses) or ideologists (bourgeois or proletarian), that has tabled the task of communism: a punctual political revolution ('the violent overthrow of the bourgeoisie lay[ing] the foundation for the sway of the proletariat');[46] and an ensuing protracted social revolution ('a revolutionary reconstitution of society at large'). 'The proletariat', Marx writes,

> will use its political supremacy to wrest, by degrees, all capital from the bourgeoisie, to centralize all instruments of production in the hands of the State, i.e., of the proletariat organized as the ruling class and to increase the total of the productive forces as rapidly as possible.[47]

In thus 'entirely revolutionizing the mode of production', what was subsequently termed the 'dictatorship of the proletariat' would witness the gradual extinction of the conditions of existence for social classes – hence of the working class itself – and therewith the dissolution not only of its own state power but of the state in general: 'In place of the old bourgeois society, with its classes and class antagonisms, we shall have an association in which the free development of each is the condition for the free development of all.'[48]

PRECURSIVE RECURSIVE

We have seen that in their Preface to the 1872 German edition of the *Manifesto* Marx and Engels reaffirmed the essential correctness of its 'general principles'. Taking their cue from the founders, their successors – revolutionary or reformist, social democratic or communist, representatives of the Second, Third or Fourth Internationals – reiterated the point. For Kautsky, drafting the theoretical section of the German SPD's Erfurt Programme, the *Manifesto* 'laid the scientific foundation of modern socialism'.[49] According to Labriola, anticipating its fiftieth anniversary, its 'model philosophy of history ... can be retouched, completed and developed, but cannot be corrected'.[50] Writing on the eve of the First World War, Lenin asserted that it 'gave an integral and systematic exposition of [Marx's] doctrine, an exposition which has remained the best to this day'.[51] Shortly after its conclusion, addressing the founding conference of the German Communist Party, Rosa Luxemburg defined the *Manifesto* as 'the great charter of our movement', and proclaimed that 'our revolution is subject to the prepotent laws of historical determinism, a law which guarantees that, despite all difficulties and complications ..., we shall nevertheless advance step by step towards our goal'.[52] The degeneration of the Third International having compounded the collapse of the Second, Trotsky, marking the *Manifesto*'s ninetieth anniversary, conceded 'the error of Marx and Engels in regard to the historical dates', while reckoning that its origin – 'an underestimation of future possibilities latent in capitalism and ... an overestimation of the revolutionary maturity of the proletariat' – had been rectified at source as it were, so that '[t]he protracted crisis of international revolution ... is reducible in essentials to the crisis of revolutionary leadership': hence the need for a Fourth International.[53] Prefacing centennial editions in 1948, the leader of the Italian Communist Party could adduce the post-war expansion of communism as proof of the *Manifesto*'s predictions, concluding that '[h]istory is marching inexorably along the road traced one hundred years ago by the titanic thought of Karl Marx and Friedrich Engels';[54] while a prominent social democratic thinker, writing on behalf of a British Labour Party likewise at the height of its post-war powers, could assert: 'Few documents in the history of mankind have stood up so remarkably to the test of verification by the future as the *Communist Manifesto*. A century after its publication, no one has been able seriously to controvert any of its major positions.'[55] Eduard Bernstein, at the turn of the nineteenth century, was virtually a lone dissenting voice, identifying the *Manifesto* as the source of the economic catastrophism he reprehended in social democratic theory, and which attested (so he argued) to the unexpurgated 'remnants of utopianism' in a professedly scientific socialism.[56]

Explicit or implicit in the *Communist Manifesto*, and as such quite legitimately distilled from it by Kautsky and Labriola, Lenin and Luxemburg, Trotsky and Togliatti, the 'scientific' conception of socialism rested on several pillars. At the risk of some unavoidable repetition, they can be delineated as follows. First, a vision of the broad trajectory of human history and a periodisation of it, from primitive communism, via various forms of class society, to advanced communism, which effected the 'expropriation of the expropriators' and sealed the end of human *pre*-history (not, contrary to Francis Fukuyama, the 'end of history' per se).

Second, a projection of the specific tendencies of the capitalist mode of production, whose contradictory dynamics created the requisite conditions for its supersession by communism. Like the modes of production that preceded it, capitalism was a transient entity, because its congenital tendency to systemic, chronic and worsening crisis rendered it unsustainable. Nevertheless, it possessed a progressive character, consisting above all in the fact that its global development of the productive forces betokened abolition of the material scarcity in which the exploitation and oppression of class society were rooted. Hence its generation of the material conditions for its replacement by the classless society of communism. But for evolution to issue into revolution, the social conditions created by capitalism were of equal salience.

The third pillar, then, was a social agency: the collective labourer produced by modern industrial capitalism with a material interest in, and a structural capacity for, transforming it. The industrial working class was the Archimedean point – but an intra-mundane one, internal to history – for overthrowing the existing order and establishing a new one, which could only be communism. The inevitability of the epochal transition from capitalism to communism did not entail its automaticity. Accomplishment of what was indeed inevitable nevertheless required a collective human agent: 'scientific socialism' appointed it.

As to that new order, it furnished the fourth pillar: the eminently feasible political objective of communal possession and direction of the means of livelihood, in a direct democracy of the associated producers.

Fifth, and finally, the Marxian–Marxist conception of socialism rested upon an ideal, however much such discourse may subsequently have been disparaged as moralism: the authentic fulfilment, in sum, of the ideals of 1789 – a synthesis of liberty, equality and solidarity, embodied in the *Manifesto*'s 'association, in which the free development of each is the condition for the free development of all'.

Whatever the innumerable, interminable later controversies between (and within) the reformist and revolutionary branches of Marxian socialism – over organisation (the institutional form of socialist politics), agency (the working class or class alliances around it), strategy (parliamentary or insurrectionary), and so on – virtual unanimity obtained for a century or more about the five pillars of what its artisans and partisans termed 'scientific socialism'. Above all, this broad consensus was grounded in an unshakable conviction as to not only the intolerability of capitalism, but also its ephemerality, which condemned it sooner or later to make way for a superior civilisation and culture. In effect, 'Comrade History' was on the side of communism. As Marx and Engels had insisted in *The German Ideology*, 'communism is not for us a *state of affairs* which is to be established, an *ideal* to which reality will [have] to adjust itself. We call communism the *real* movement which abolishes the present state of things. The conditions of this movement result from the now existing premise.'[57]

TERRA INFIRMA

'History is the judge – its executioner, the proletarian,' Marx declared in his 1856 speech.[58] Weighed against such imposing historical optimism, how does the 'spectre of communism' brandished in the *Manifesto* shape up today?

In the aftermath of the neo-liberal offensive of the 1980s, it is that optimism about the future which has been lost. To put it no higher, the problems of the organisation, agency, strategy and goal of a systemic alternative remain unsolved, suggesting (contra the 1859 Preface) that the mere ability to table a task does not ensure its resolution. Moreover, they are dramatised by the crying discrepancy between the faits accomplis of capitalism and the faits inaccomplis of socialism, in the twentieth century; between the prevalence of capitalism, verifying the main premise of the *Manifesto*, and the absence of communism, infirming its consequent; or between what Marx called the 'poetry of the future' and what (following Merleau-Ponty) we might call the 'prose of the world'. The fact – 'palpable, overwhelming and not to be controverted', in Marx's words – is that organisation, agency and strategy have nowhere been conjugated to attain the stipulated goal. The predictable upshot has been to discredit both the desirability of a socialist alternative (given the record of Stalinism and social democracy) and its feasibility (given the non-corroboration of the classical conception of it). The argument from dystopia – socialism equals Stalinism, the worst of all possible worlds – is reinforced by the argument from utopia – socialism equals an impracticable ideal, an impossible best of all possible worlds.

KARL MARX

In an essay dating from 1971, Eric Hobsbawm observed of the class of '68 that:

> There is ... one major difference between the new revolutionism and that of my generation between the wars. We had ... hope and a concrete model of the alternative society: socialism. Today this faith in the great October revolution and the Soviet Union has largely disappeared ... and nothing has replaced it. ... What has taken the place of our perspective is a combination of negative hatred of the existing society and Utopia.[59]

Whether Hobsbawm's 'combination' does justice to its subject is a question we may leave hanging. But that it captures something of contemporary anti-capitalism in the 'alter-globalisation' movement seems undeniable. In brief, socialism has, to all intents and purposes, become utopian once again. Not necessarily in the most pejorative of the received senses – namely, a hortatory rhetoric counter-posing a pristine socialist ideal to a degraded capitalist reality – but in as much as (to vary Marx's claim) history is the judge – and capitalism (to date, at any rate) the executioner.

In other words, if the *Communist Manifesto* retains an astonishing 'actuality' as regards contemporary capitalism, this has something profoundly paradoxical about it. On the one hand, much of what, 150 years ago, was no more than an astonishing anticipation of the revolutionary vocation of capitalism, has been – is every day being – confirmed before our very eyes. Capitalism,

25

if not the bourgeoisie, is creating a world after its own image, battering down most (if not all) Chinese walls with the heavy artillery of commodities, giving free rein to the simultaneously creative, destructive and self-destructive forces inherent in it. On the other hand, as the Italian Marxist philosopher Domenico Losurdo has underscored in his re-edition of the *Manifesto*, this very 'actuality' – what renders the pamphlet of much more than merely antiquarian or academic interest – is the 'symptom of a defeat':[60] the vanquishing of the 'historical movement' to which Marx and Engels intended to give theoretical expression, and whose practical triumph they expected as the revolutionary bourgeoisie suffered the sorcerer's fate.

In effect, as Hobsbawm among others has argued, the *Manifesto* is structured around a kind of implicit syllogism, derived from the materialist conception of history, that deduces the advent of communism from the insuperably contradictory dynamic of capitalism.[61] Even if the premises – the fatal suicidal tendencies of capitalism and the 'universal' vocation of the proletariat – were correct, they would not entail the all-important conclusion that the future of capitalism, however immediate or distant, is communism. In the event, as noted above, not only Marx and Engels, but also their immediate successors acknowledged the possibility of 'the common ruin of the contending classes'. 'As things stand today,' Kautsky warned in 1892, 'capitalist civilization cannot continue; we must either move forward into socialism or fall back into barbarism.'[62]

Yet the very prospect of such a historical regression was adduced, without further ado, as conclusive proof of the necessity and hence inevitability of communism – for example, in Luxemburg's formulation of the socialism or barbarism alternative in 1918.[63]

Trotsky almost put his finger on the neuralgic point in 1937, only to obviate it by resorting to 'the crisis of revolutionary leadership'. As a founding document of Marxism, the *Communist Manifesto over*estimated the potential of the industrial working class in direct proportion to its *under*estimation of the potential of capitalism. Lenin had observed in 1913 that '[t]he chief thing in the doctrine of Marx is that it brings out the historic role of the proletariat as the builder of socialist society. Marx first advanced it in 1844.'[64] Marx's nomination of the proletariat as the 'universal class', made in the Introduction to *A Critique of Hegel's Philosophy of Right*,[65] predated his anatomy of industrial capitalist society, but was thereafter superimposed on it in the materialist conception of history. The upshot was the equation of a philosophical class – the proletariat – destined to redeem the whole of humanity from the alienation of its 'species-being' in class society, with an economic class – industrial wage-labourers – motivated, in the transition from a class in-itself to a class for-itself, to emancipate itself from the exploitation of capitalist society. On the basis of that equation, Marx and Engels could claim in *The Holy Family* (1845) that '[i]t is not a question of what this or that proletarian, or even the whole proletariat, at the moment *regards* as its aim. It is a question of *what the proletariat is*, and what, in accordance with this *being*, it will historically be compelled to do.'[66]

Any hesitations or second thoughts on Marx's part about the ultimate soundness of his theory of history, which may be glimpsed from particular qualifications subsequently entered by him, not to mention his abstention from completing and publishing Volumes 2 and 3 of *Capital* (let alone embarking on the others), were pretty much discounted by Engels, who was the true founder of the Marxism bequeathed to the Second International. With *Anti-Dühring* and the 1859 Preface as their Bible, Kautsky and co. did precisely what Marx had occasion to remonstrate against in a letter dating from 1877, 'using as [their] master key a general historico-philosophical theory, the supreme virtue of which consists in being supra-historical'.[67]

According to the Marxist prospectus of the late nineteenth century, socialism was of course to be expected in what the *Manifesto* referred to as 'the leading civilized countries' – the developed capitalist world of Western Europe and North America – whose '[u]nited action is one of the first conditions for the emancipation of the proletariat'.[68] When the bankruptcy of the Kautskyist orthodoxy of ends became plain in 1914, Lenin switched the spatio-temporal coordinates of socialist revolution from capitalism as such to imperialism as its 'highest' (or latest) stage, from the strongest to the 'weakest links' of the capitalist chain, from 'advanced' to 'backward' countries – in short, from West to East. He therewith effected a radical break with the received Eurocentric antithesis between 'civilised' and 'barbarian' countries, retained (in heavily qualified fashion) by Marx and Engels, and promoted by social democratic supporters of imperialism's *mission civilisatrice*, from Bernstein to Brown.[69] In this sense – which is *not* to condemn it – October 1917 represented not merely a revolt against the *Communist Manifesto* and the 1859 Preface, but (as Gramsci rightly saw) a 'revolution against *Capital*' – against its conception of 'the natural laws of capitalist production ... working themselves out with iron necessity', such that 'capitalist production begets, with the inexorability of a natural process, its own negation'.[70] The late Marx had himself envisaged the prospect of a specifically Russian road to communism; and the Preface to the 1882 Russian edition of the *Manifesto*, while confirming that it 'had as its object the proclamation of the inevitably impending dissolution of modern bourgeois property', had allowed for the possibility of a 'Russian Revolution becom[ing] a signal for a proletarian revolution in the West, so that both complement each other'.[71] For Lenin and Trotsky, unlike Stalin and Mao, 'proletarian revolution in the West', 'signalled' by revolution in the East, was a precondition for the very survival of the latter. And about the 'inevitably impending dissolution' of capitalism in the West, in the 'era of wars and revolutions' that had dawned with 1914, they harboured few doubts.

For mirroring the inter-modal capacity of the Western proletariat – its ability to effect a transition from the capitalist to the communist mode of production, 'increas[ing] the total of the productive forces as rapidly as possible' – was the class incapacity of the Western bourgeoisie to develop those forces any further. By the gauge of the 1859 Preface and *Capital*, the developed capitalist world was, as it came to be put, 'rotten-ripe' for the proletarian revolution that would release socialised productive forces from their private capitalist 'integument'. An easy enough mistake to make between the wars, capitalism was obviously no more doomed than communism was fated. Plausible enough at the time, economic catastrophism – especially in the shape of the so-called *Zusammensbruchstheorie* (the theory of capitalism's inevitable collapse) – proved a singularly poor guide to economic reality thereafter. Post-1945, notwithstanding its social and environmental costs and recurrent crises, global capitalism was to prove capable of a quite prodigious development of the productive forces, quantitative and qualitative; and, in the developed world at least, compatible with rising living standards amounting to unparalleled prosperity. Therewith it did not so much integrate the industrial working class in the West as 'disintegrate' it.[72] If it has not quite buried it, the sorcerer (to revert to Marx's metaphors) has prepared the grave of its putative gravedigger.

Even if, when and where the stipulated conditions for a transition from capitalism have been assembled, they have turned out to be quite insufficient. This does not entail that capitalism is eternal (its indivisibly creative–destructive animal spirits, detected by Marx, might mean that the sorcerer is digging his own grave, enacting the scenario of a 'common ruin'). Nor does it entail that, in some unforeseeable eventuality, a form of socialism will not supervene in the future (after all, as de Gaulle once remarked, 'the future lasts a long time'). What it does entail is that the particular form of its inscription in history by 'scientific socialism' can only be said not to have been falsified in as much as, on Popperian or Lakatosian grounds, falsification is indefinitely deferrable. Yet this is cold comfort. For what can in turn be concluded from it is that, whatever else it may be, Marxian–Marxist socialism is not scientific in the sense in which the overwhelming majority of its adherents believed it to be.

The adjective 'Marxian–Marxist' is used advisedly above. Although the rich complexity of Marx's immense oeuvre is such as to render him the first (and greatest) of the Marxist heretics, the ideological formation that was historical Marxism – the official party Marxism of the Second, Third and Fourth Internationals alike – was no mere betrayal of his thought. It was a possible extrapolation from one major tendency of it, which easily withstood attempted reformations, in the spirit of a different Marx, by such as Lukács and Althusser.

The passe-partout Marx repudiated in 1877 was in at least some measure – arguably good – cut by him.

In sum, historical Marxism itself projected a utopian socialism, albeit not in the sense of 'writing recipes ... for the cook-shops of the future'.[73] Why? As Costanzo Preve has compellingly argued in a series of works,[74] from the start it secreted three defining characteristics that it retained, to varying degrees, for the duration of its career. The first was historicism: the implication of a linear, progressive, providential historical time eventually realising an immanent design – a teleological conception of history as a process with an origin (alienation), a meta-subject (the proletariat), and a goal (communism). The second was economism: charging the growth of the productive forces with the task of preparing the future – the end of human pre-history – by inducing the emergence of the class-subject whose 'historical mission' was to secure it. The third was utopianism: the conviction that the self-subversive dialectic of the capitalist mode of production would in and of itself vouchsafe the conditions for the constitution of a form of human society that could directly satisfy human needs, dispensing with political state and economic market. Hence the repeated injunctions in the Marxist tradition against superfluous, speculative blueprinting of a predestined *Zukunftstaat* that was destined not to arrive.

Latent in the *Communist Manifesto*, if not patent, these three cornerstones of historical Marxism were the articles of faith of nothing less than a secularised and sociologised 'religion of the subaltern', as Gramsci put it.[75] In this regard at any rate, contrary to the claim of a prominent British Marxist welcoming the birth of a new anti-capitalist movement at Seattle at the close of the twentieth century, a pamphlet published in the mid nineteenth century is not 'a manifesto for it'.[76]

In his splendid account of the European left, Geoff Eley writes that '[i]n 1848, Marx radically misread the signs. As Engels ruefully acknowledged, what he mistook for capitalism's death-throes were actually its birth pangs.'[77] In defiance of Hegel's instruction, the Owl of Minerva took wing at dawn and spelt out the signs of end times. A century and a half on, with dusk yet to fall, it is clear that, in more ways than one, this sense of an ending was only the beginning.

TWO

Full Spectrum Dominance? Francis Fukuyama

Where the 1980s unleashed a humble prefix (post-) on Western intellectual culture, the 1990s deluged the planet with the G word, releasing a veritable torrent of globalarrhoea. Faced with the truisms (or untruisms) of the age, it was tempting to adopt the stance of Jane Austen's Elinor, who 'agreed to it all, for it did not seem worth the compliment of rational opposition'. In any case, intimations of mortality were ubiquitous: the end of an era was an era of endings. According to a certain apocalyptic litany, the last quarter-century of the second millennium AD delivered a quietus to the Cold War and communism, the working class and Fordism, the Enlightenment project and modernity, the nation-state and sovereignty, and so on *ad libitum*.

If any one text captured this endist Zeitgeist, it was superficially the most extravagant of them all – a brief article published in the summer of 1989 by the then deputy director of the US State Department's policy planning staff. Francis Fukuyama's 'The End of History?' predated the earthquake in the East. In retrospect, however, the safety catch of its question mark may be regarded as equivalent to the Webbs', in the first edition of their *Soviet Communism: A New Civilisation*. Three years later, when a full-blown version of what had in the interim become known as the 'Fukuyama thesis' appeared, the punctuation mark had duly been retired from the title – ample evidence that the thesis boiled down to an equation which, if not simple, was single: the end of communism = the end of socialism = the end of history. It was replaced by an initially inscrutable formula – 'and the Last Man' – whose precise bearing on the equation was tricked out in the final part of the book.

PROSPECTS

Of late, if not having second thoughts as such, Fukuyama has been entering qualifications and clarifications. In an Afterword to the second, 2006 edition of *The End of History and the Last Man*, he is at pains to stress that his essay in substantive philosophy of history was in fact 'a theory of modernization that raised the question of where that modernization process would ultimately lead'.[1] Of even greater moment,

> One misunderstanding I do want to clarify ...
> concerns the very widespread misapprehension that
> I was somehow arguing for a specifically American
> version of the end of history.... Many have taken the

end of history to be a brief for American hegemony
over the rest of the world, not just in the realm of
ideas and values, but through the actual exercise
of American power to order the world according
to American interests.

Nothing could be further from the truth. ...
the European Union is a much fuller real-world
embodiment of the concept than is the contemporary
United States.[2]

Fuelled by the debacle in Iraq, Fukuyama's anxiety
to allay any such 'misapprehension' is evident from
his return to it, in a syndicated newspaper column
in April 2007, where he repudiates the notion that
'coercive regime change was ... the key to democratic
transition'.[3] The previous year, in a book whose US title
(and UK subtitle) blithely assimilates two continents to
one country, in a common linguistic symptom of the
syndrome it indignantly disavows, Fukuyama advocated
a 'realistic Wilsonianism' for US foreign policy, as an
antidote to the unrealistic neo-conservatism allegedly
responsible for the despatch of armed missionaries
to Iraq.[4] The position he had defended in 1992 was
demarcated from the political and social engineering
of Wolfowitz et al., on the grounds that the latter, as
was readily predictable from its ideocratic impulses and
revolutionary designs, generated negative unintended
consequences. However well intentioned, it was
counter-productive. Counter to what? The very Project
for the New American Century of which Fukuyama
was a co-founder. The dispute, in short, revolved

around variable means to an identical end. Fukuyama did not so much declare against US 'unilateralism' and 'hard power' as urge a judicious hybrid of them with 'multilateralism' and 'soft power', to create a common-or-Garton Ash variety more readily digestible by the 'International Community'.

How does this square with the original argument? Was it an exercise in modernisation theory, reducible to the postulate that the desire for prosperity is universal and that, all things being equal, it will ultimately issue in democracy? Was it clearly distinguishable – and correspondingly distinguished – from any 'brief for American hegemony' and 'coercive regime change'? And however that may be, how does it stand up today?

To take the pre-lapsarian statement of 1989 first, the thesis ran roughly as follows. Twentieth-century history was turning 'full circle', from the collapse of Western liberalism in the First World War to its impending victory in the Cold War: not the 'end of ideology' announced by the modernisation theorists of the 1950s and 1960s, discerning a convergence between industrial societies, capitalist and socialist, but 'an unabashed victory of economic and political liberalism'.[5] The 'triumph of the West, of the Western *idea*', betokened 'the end of history as such: that is, the end point of mankind's ideological evolution and the universalization of Western liberal democracy as the final form of human government'.[6] Beckoning humanity was a '"Common Marketization" of world politics' – or, alternatively put, 'liberal democracy in the political sphere combined with easy access to VCRs and stereos in the economic'.[7] Following Hegel, 'the history of the World is none other than the progress of the consciousness of Freedom' and its realisation.[8] That consciousness was prevailing, as attested by 'the total exhaustion of viable systemic alternatives to Western liberalism'.[9] This had concluded history, not in the trivially untrue sense of bringing empirical events to an abrupt halt, but in as much as it had realised its goal: freedom. What we were witnessing was not a cessation but a culmination: to mobilise two Americanisms, end times were quality time.

In a way, then, the end of history *was* the end of ideology, because it comprised the consummation of one universal ideology. Upper-case History, construed by Fukuyama as a *Kampfplatz* between contending ideologies, 'embodied' (so he stipulated) 'in important social or political forces and movements, ... which are therefore part of world history',[10] had arrived at its destination. Contrary to Plekhanov's classical Marxist assurance that '[w]e, indeed, know our way and are seated in the historical train which at full speed takes us to our goal',[11] the locomotive of history had terminated not at the Finland Station, but at a hypermarket. All roads lead to Disneyland?

Given Fukuyama's conception of 'History', the myriad malcontents of post-historical civilisation, whatever their visibility or volubility, constituted no challenge to it. The 'strange thoughts occur[ring] to people in Albania or Burkina Faso' carried little weight,[12] for they were impotent before the trend line of the times: a 'universal homogeneous state' of liberal democratic capitalism from which system-threatening antagonisms had been eliminated. Contra Hegel, the Earth formed a sphere and liberal history was describing a circle around it. This was not a Panglossian prospect. While liberalism represented the best practicable economic and political world, it was not perfect. But it provided the ineluctable framework for solving such remaining human ills as were soluble. With the defeat of fascism at mid century and communism at its close, and given the intrinsic frailty of religion and nationalism as alternative poles of attraction, there were no serious – 'world-historical' – competitors still in the field.

The elegiac note struck in conclusion to the article, in a passage reproduced on the back cover of the book, supplies an initial gauge of the gulf between this philosophy of history and any theory of modernisation:

> The end of history will be a very sad time. The struggle for recognition, the willingness to risk one's life for a purely abstract goal, the worldwide ideological struggle that called forth daring, courage, imagination, and idealism, will be replaced by economic calculation, the endless solving of technical problems, environmental concerns, and the satisfaction of sophisticated consumer demands.[13]

Purged of the 'struggle for recognition' that drove history to its end point, condemned to a civilisation stamped with the spiritual vices of its material benefits, perhaps humanity, if only *pour se désennuyer*, would restart the historical process.

Attributed to Hegel, whom Marx had mistakenly inverted to yield a historical materialism fantasising 'a communist utopia that would finally resolve all prior contradictions',[14] the proximate source of Fukuyama's 'idealist' conception of history was of course Alexandre Kojève. His interpretation of *The Phenomenology of Spirit*, foregrounding the master–slave dialectic, extrapolated the 'struggle for recognition' that furnishes the motor of history on Fukuyama's reading of it. For Kojève, as for Hegel, 'world history' was the relevant tribunal: *Die Weltgeschichte ist das Weltgericht*.[15] But its destination was switched, from the differentiated freedom of the liberal–constitutional state to 'the universal and homogeneous State'. And its locus shifted, from expeditionary France (the spirit of Napoleon) to revolutionary Russia (the spectre of Stalin) and thence, via an evolving EEC (shades of Monnet), back again. In a subsequent note, as Fukuyama remarks, Kojève identified the consumerist and incipiently classless USA as the paradigm of the homogeneity toward which history was tending.[16]

Across the political spectrum, from Samuel Huntington to Eric Hobsbawm,[17] or from Bernard-Henri Lévy to Jacques Derrida, the reception of Fukuyama's article was frequently negative. Aside from a pervasive misapprehension, derived from a passing inacquaintance with the text, that Fukuyama was arguing precisely what he was not – namely, that events had ceased – the most common objection was to the very project of a philosophy of history. In the Anglophone world nothing was less congenial to indigenous empiricism or domesticated postmodernism. Fukuyama's resurrection of a Hegelian variant of it – by Lyotardian criteria, grand narrative of speculation and emancipation par excellence – brought down upon his head accusations of metaphysics. Worse, in so far as he had reversed Marx's inversion of Hegel's philosophy of history, preserving its theoretical structure while according primacy to ideology and changing the historical terminus to capitalism, he stood convicted of an 'inverted Marxism'.

Undeterred by this, and by support on precisely such grounds from Perry Anderson,[18] Fukuyama proceeded to an exposition and defence of his thesis. In the process, he significantly complicated it.

RESULTS?

Distinguishing, in his Introduction, between 'history' – 'the occurrence of events' – and 'History' – 'a single, coherent, evolutionary process' – Fukuyama at once disposed of a prevalent ingenuous criticism of his thesis.[19] The question it addressed and the answer it returned were these:

> Whether, at the end of the twentieth century, it makes sense ... once again to speak of a coherent and directional History of mankind that will eventually lead the greater part of humanity to liberal democracy. The answer I arrive at is yes, for two separate reasons. One has to do with economics, and the other has to do with what is termed the 'struggle for recognition.'[20]

Thus, Fukuyama now posited not one but two motors of his 'Universal History', combining trans-historical 'material' and 'ideological' mechanisms of social transformation. The first – developed in Part 2 – was the 'logic of modern natural science', which entailed a 'universal evolution in the direction of capitalism',[21] given the indubitable superiority of the latter in satisfying material desires. Itself an economic theory of historical change, unlike the Marxist version it posted capitalism – not communism – as its 'final result'.[22] However, 'economic modernization' was insufficient for the advent of democracy and hence of political liberalism. To realise that goal, a different mechanism had to be posited, yielding a 'second, parallel account of the historical process' in Part 3.[23]

Whence the imperative to return to Hegel – or rather (as Fukuyama concedes), turn to 'a new, synthetic philosopher named Hegel–Kojève'[24] – for a non-materialist philosophy of history rooted in the 'struggle for recognition', which is itself based by Fukuyama (not Kojève) on Plato's theory of the soul (in particular, *thymos* or 'spiritedness').[25] The 'desire for recognition' supposedly supplied the 'missing link between liberal economics and liberal politics',[26] creating the sufficient condition for the conjunction of capitalism (satisfaction of material needs) and liberal democracy (satisfaction of the desire for recognition) that is the end of history as such. Consequently, it was 'the motor of history', allocated explanatory primacy, not merely a second motor assigned co-determinacy.[27]

Thus far, it might be thought, Part 2 is going to offer a version of Marx minus communism, and Part 3 a version of Hegel plus democracy, with the latter 'sublating' the former in suitably Hegelian style. However, in raising likely objections to his thesis from left and right, Fukuyama introduced a third figure, fleetingly glimpsed in the conclusion to the article: Nietzsche. Rebutting the left's denial that capitalist democracy affords 'universal and reciprocal recognition' on account of its inherent inequalities, Fukuyama pondered a Nietzschean line of critique:

> Is not the man who is completely satisfied by nothing more than universal and equal recognition something less than a full human being, indeed, an object of contempt, a 'last man' with neither striving nor aspiration? Is there not a side of the human personality that ... [will] remain unfulfilled by the 'peace and prosperity' of contemporary liberal democracy?[28]

Were that to be the case, Nietzsche would emerge as *tertium gaudens*, with *megalothymia* (the desire to be recognised as superior) trumping *isothymia* (the desire to be recognised as equal), thereby negating Hegel and Marx alike and obstructing any end of history in an apotheosis of 'slave morality'.

Such troubling questions were deferred to Part 5. Meanwhile, marshalling empirical evidence for the victory of 'the liberal *idea*' as 'the single universal standard', with the collapse of communism and assorted authoritarianisms,[29] Fukuyama posed the question – is there an alternative that is superior to it? – and replied with a resounding TINA. The challenge of Islam – soon to be inflated beyond all rational measure by ex-Cold warriors at risk of superannuation – was coolly discounted.[30] For their part, Western consumerates could not imagine a world at once different and better from the capitalist democracy they inhabited; while those currently outside its pale aspired only to *droit de cité* within it. These considerations licensed the project of 'a Universal History of mankind in the direction of liberal democracy'.[31] Yet while the 'mechanism of desire', powered by instrumental reason, 'in some way makes capitalism inevitable',[32] it did not guarantee liberal democracy. To be sure, there was 'a very strong correlation' between economic liberalisation and political democratisation,[33] attributed by modernisation theory to the creation of middles classes seeking political rights. But an empirical correlation was not a causal connection. And if the material mechanism was, in an image reminiscent of Plekhanov, the 'locomotive of history',[34] if unbounded accumulation was humanity's overriding priority, then 'the truly winning combination would appear to be neither liberal democracy nor socialism ... , but the combination of liberal economics and authoritarian politics'.[35] A directional Universal History cast in economic–materialist terms might with equal – possibly greater – plausibility yield an authoritarian conclusion as a liberal one. The end of history would still be capitalism, only not of the Western but of the Eastern variety – Singapore rather than the USA. Understandably referred to by Fukuyama only in the context of its communist revolution, China today might be cited as an imposing instance, of a quite different magnitude, of the species.

In reality, because *homo oeconomicus* is not the whole man, 'a kind of Marxist interpretation of history ... lead[ing] to a completely non-Marxist conclusion'[36] was inadequate. Complementing the material mechanism, but more profound than it, 'the primary motor of human history is ... a totally non-economic drive, the *struggle for recognition*'.[37] With the resolution of that struggle in the synthesis of Hegel–Kojève's master–slave dialectic constituted by equal recognition, economic and political freedom was conjoined in a 'universal–homogeneous state':

> The universal and homogeneous state that appears at the end of history can thus be seen as resting on the *twin pillars* of economics and recognition.

> The human historical process that leads up to it
> has been driven forward *equally* by the progressive
> unfolding of modern natural science and by the
> struggle for recognition.[38]

Here the material mechanism and the ideological
mechanism have become co-determinants, with the
logical consequence that the latter is depicted as
'a major driver' rather than 'the primary motor'.
Consequently, space is left open for the kind of 'bureaucratic–authoritarian future'[39] arguably intimated by
the Kojèvian – and decidedly non-Hegelian – formula
of the 'universal–homogeneous state' itself.

In any case, does this state satisfy 'spiritual' as well
as material desire? Is the master's *megalothymia* successfully sublimated in it even as the slave's *isothymia*
is fulfilled? What is not in doubt for Fukuyama is the
ongoing, post-historical role of *thymos*: 'Even at the
end of history, some form of irrational *thymos* is still
necessary ... to keep our rational, liberal economic world
going, or at least if we are to be in the front rank of
world economic powers.'[40] In this regard, the 'highly
atomistic economic liberalism of the U.S. or Britain'
– the 'we' Fukuyama doubtless has in mind – might
prove inferior to more communitarian varieties of
capitalism.[41] For radical individualism undermines the
solidaristic group ethic on which continued economic
success seems to be built. Once again, Asian societies
that conjugated economic liberalism and 'paternalistic

authoritarianism' potentially mounted a potent challenge to 'liberal universalism'.[42]

Given that in Fukuyama's most optimistic scenario, the geopolitical world would remain divided for some time to come along post-historical and historical lines – fault-lines – the issue of what Kojève had brusquely defined as 'the alignment of the provinces'[43] needed to be dealt with. In humanity's progress 'toward a pacific union', post-historical countries would share an interest 'in protecting themselves from external threat, and in promoting the cause of democracy where it does not exist'.[44] Since such societies invariably comported themselves peacefully, 'the U.S. and other democracies have a long-term interest in preserving the sphere of democracy in the world, and in expanding it where possible and prudent'.[45] Suitably tempered by considerations of feasibility and prudence, the 'traditional moralism of American foreign policy', sponsoring 'human rights and "democratic values"' (nothing so vulgar as capitalism, apparently), was not inappropriate.[46] At any rate, 'realism' in international affairs was now a fallacious doctrine, as both description and prescription.

What of the 'realm of freedom' thus made or in the making? Did the 'discontents' of democracy warrant a book of lamentations, Marxist or Nietzschean? At stake here was not whether 'capitalist liberal democracy'[47] contained serious problems – that it most certainly did – but whether these were contradictions of such severity as to frustrate its claim to represent the end of history. While the left targeted the social inequality between classes belying a formal equality of citizens, the right trained its fire on a spurious denial of natural human inequality in an artificially imposed civic equality.

The persistence of 'major social inequalities' in even the best liberal society was undeniable, derived from the incorrigible 'tension between the principles of liberty and equality' on which liberal societies are founded.[48] But such inequalities did not contradict those principles; they merely indicated that there was a 'trade-off' between them.[49] And rare were the left-wing critics of liberalism today who proposed to jettison its principles in the endeavour to remedy its inequalities. Indeed, any future challenge from the left might be expected to crystallise in the guise of excessive liberal egalitarianism, gratuitously and recklessly multiplying demands for the recognition of rights, not necessarily human. A little difference could go a very long way.

Enter Nietzsche and the right-wing critique of liberal democratic modernity. In seeking to repress *megalothymia*, the liberal democratic state did not embody a viable synthesis of the moralities of master and slave, but awarded the palm to the latter. Agreeing that *megalothymia* was ineradicable as the source of much that is distinctively human about *homo sapiens*, elevating it above the level of just another animal species, Fukuyama looked to its optimal sublimation in the liberal order. If given its head, *megalothymia* could be expected to operate as a subversive force. But if not given its due, 'an excess of *isothymia* – ... the fanatical desire for equal recognition' – loomed,[50] corrosive of community. Inspection of the USA suggested that such fanaticism posed a greater threat than surplus *megalothymia*. Yet even if 'those who remain dissatisfied [with liberty and equality] will always have the potential to restart history',[51] Fukuyama could close with a seemingly upbeat reaffirmation of 'the fact that history is being driven in a coherent direction by rational desire and rational recognition ... and the fact that liberal democracy in reality constitutes the best possible solution to the human problem'.[52]

Starting out from Fukuyama's reflections on the dilemmas confronting Lockean Anglo-liberalism, Joseph McCarney detected the presence of a conservative 'esoteric' doctrine in *The End of History and the Last Man*, traceable to Leo Strauss, which ill accords with its 'exoteric' doctrine: a critique of US-style liberal democracy as opposed to an apologia for it.[53] For Alex Callinicos, Fukuyama's quite explicit doctrine is to be located where Fukuyama had himself effectively stationed it – within the reactionary tradition of *Kulturkritik* that took shape in the aftermath of the French Revolution, and whose foremost representative is Nietzsche.[54] In either event, the precise contours and corresponding evaluation of the end state become more imponderable than they seem at first sight.

Depending on whether Fukuyama's 'parallel' histories of desire and recognition converge on the same conclusion or, alternatively, diverge at some point; and according to our assessment of that conclusion, four possible outcomes might be envisaged:

(1) US liberal democratic capitalism represents the end of history and, for all its tares, is to be welcomed as optimal. This was how many of his critics received the Fukuyama thesis, but its author dissociates himself from it in his 2006 Afterword.

(2) Asian authoritarian-paternalistic capitalism is the end of history, falling short politically but more than making the grade economically. This could be inferred from Fukuyama's allusion to the 'truly winning combination' in his book.

(3) European liberal democratic capitalism is the end of history, prefiguring a 'Common Marketization' of geopolitics. Indicated in the 2006 Afterword, this had been hinted at in Fukuyama's original article.

(4) 'History' has not been concluded, as a result of the presence of contradictions in liberalism that continue to drive the historical process. None of (1) – (3) obtains, because each of them – as a result of the capitalism, the liberal democracy, or both – fails fully to satisfy humanity's material needs and/or its desire for recognition. This argument can assume either a left- or a right-wing form.

The logic of Fukuyama's argument points to (1) or (3) as his option – significantly modulated, however, by the induction of elements of *Kulturkritik* that convey his ambivalence about post-historical civilisation. After all, 'the end of history will be a very sad time'.

MYSTICAL SHELL

When, in his Postface to the second edition of *Capital* Volume 1, Marx sought to specify his relationship to the Hegelian dialectic, he famously contended that by 'inverting' it he had 'discover[ed] the rational kernel within the mystical shell'.[55] We shall attempt an analogous operation with the Hegelian–Kojèvian dialectic of Fukuyama, starting with the mystical shell.

Fukuyama maintains that his philosophy of history, unlike its Hegelian predecessor, is not a 'secular theodicy' – 'a justification of all that exists in terms of history's final end'.[56] Yet it manifestly is teleological:

> The particular events of history can become meaningful only with respect to some larger end or goal, the achievement of which necessarily brings the historical process to a close. This final end of man is what makes all particular events potentially intelligible.[57]

As such, Universal History is obliged 'to discard entire peoples and times as essentially pre- or non-historical, because they do not bear on the central "plot" of his or her story'.[58]

Meaning/story: the words have been let slip. Fukuyama not only advances a theory of historical change – something any candidate for the title of theory of history must do. He constructs a historical teleology, offering an account of the overall meaning of the human story provided by its goal (the state of affairs in which it culminates). *Le sens de l'Histoire*, in the dual French acceptation of *sens* (direction and meaning), explains the succession of social forms that make up the content of the historical process; and therewith vindicates it. History is a process with a subject (humanity) and a goal (the universal–homogeneous state), whose developments are to be explained and evaluated, in a retrospective benefaction, by their contribution to the realisation of that goal. It is only a short step, if any, from teleology to theodicy. And it is perhaps no accident, as they used to say, if Fukuyama has casual resort to theological terminology when referring to 'the Promised Land of liberal democracy'.[59]

Readers may have registered the Althusserian accents of the preceding paragraph. Althusserian Marxism criticised orthodox historical materialism, with its epic tale of the forward march of the productive forces towards an inevitable communism, precisely on the basis that it was a 'materialist' inversion of Hegel's philosophy of history, starring the Ruse of Economic Reason and secreting a mystical kernel within a technological shell. Misconstrued thus, *Capital* was the 'Book in which the Second International read the fatality of the advent of socialism as if in a Bible'.[60] For

Althusser the abiding vice of philosophies of history lay in their ineliminably narrative structure, which plotted a story with a hero and an appointed end. Literally telling stories, they were indeed speculative meta-narratives.

Just as the founding gesture of Althusserianism was rejection of the Stalinist prolongation of the philosophy of history in a right-Hegelian version, so too it refused the alternative of a left-Hegelian variant by way of anti-Stalinist response. Moreover, as early as 1950 Althusser had declined a central principle of the Hegelo-Marxism nourished by Kojève and others' anthropological reading of *The Phenomenology*: the end of history. Invoking Marx's 1859 Preface to *A Contribution to the Critique of Political Economy*, Althusser maintained that he had conceived communism as the end of human 'pre-history' – historically determinate exploitation and alienation – and the beginning of an authentically human universal history; *not* as the end of history – some realm from which the dialectic and contradictions would have vanished, ushering in eternal harmony.[61]

The first aspect of Fukuyama's mystical shell, then, is what Althusser identified as the mystical kernel of Hegelo-Marxism, and which is retained in Fukuyama's inversion of the inversion: the very notion that History harbours goals present in germ at the origin and progressively realises them. A second area of contention – more applicable to the original article than the subsequent book – concerns Fukuyama's understanding of 'contradiction'. Frequently for him, unlike Hegel and Marx, contradictions are exogenous to systems, not endogenous to them. The relevant contradictions are inter-systemic – between, say, fascism and liberalism – as opposed to intra-systemic – within, say, capitalism. Consequently, the transition from a bi-polar world system, structured by the antagonism between capitalism and formerly existing socialism, is read as an elimination of significant contradictions. A certain historical myopia takes the exception – the post-war composition of capitalist differences for the pursuit of the 'great contest' with communism – as the norm. Yet communism was one product of – a response to – a capitalist ascendancy so riven by contradictions as to plunge the world into two cataclysmic wars in the space of twenty-five years. If Fukuyama is able to exclude intra-capitalist contradictions from his panorama, it is through the sleight of hand whereby fascism is substantially equated with communism via the Cold War topos of 'totalitarianism' and both are counter-posed to capitalism. This conveniently dis-simulates the reality that fascism was in fact a general tendency of pre-war capitalism, eliciting Horkheimer's pointed dictum: those who do not wish to speak of capitalism should keep silent about fascism.

But what exactly does Fukuyama's end state refer to? He tends to use the terms 'liberalism', 'capital-ism', 'liberal democracy', 'liberal society', 'Western societies', 'democracy', and even 'capitalist liberal democracy' interchangeably, implying that they are straightforwardly synonymous, when patently they are not. As his own parallel histories, let alone the empirical record, indicate, the conjunction between capitalism and modern representative democracy is contingent, not necessary; complex, not unitary. Suffice it to say that 'capitalist democracy' is a contradiction in terms: a type of financial oligarchy sanctioned by periodic plebiscites. At the level of a *res publica* that is ever more *privata*, the slaves have become their own masters in only the most exiguous of senses.[62]

RATIONAL KERNEL

Fukuyama may be an unreliable guide, inter alia, to Marx (and Hegel), the career of historical communism, and the democratic qualities of capitalist society. However, most criticisms of him centred elsewhere – on his substantive thesis.

Taxed with a utopianism that imagined a liberal–capitalist cornucopia where hell on earth persisted, Fukuyama can be acquitted of the charge. The end of history projected by him staked no claim to being an ideal order. As Perry Anderson argued in a commanding essay, Fukuyama's

> schema did not require the suppression of every significant social conflict or the solution of every major institutional problem. It simply asserted that liberal capitalism is the *ne plus ultra* of political and

economic life on earth. The end of history is not the arrival of a perfect system, but the elimination of any better alternatives to this one.[63]

Accordingly, the thesis is quite compatible with the persistence, even exacerbation, of problems in the liberal–capitalist global system, within and between the nation-states into which it remains organised. However complacent about these – growing inequalities, environmental perils, serial wars – and their likely intensification, Fukuyama may still be right that there is no *non*-capitalist alternative, at once feasible and desirable, to them. It would be a false consolation (not to say a defective argument) to infer from the existence of capitalist crisis some anti-capitalist resolution of it.

Detractors are therefore obliged to demonstrate the cogency of systemic alternatives discounted by Fukuyama. Of the possible contenders, two – contemporary nationalism and religious fundamentalism – were dismissed by him; and rightly so. By definition, the former is non-universal, while the latter is a sublimated form of it. Even where the 'alignment of the provinces' is proving more intractable than Kojève's telling phrase foresaw, they afford no real systemic challenge to the metropolis. To borrow the terminology of UK parking restrictions, they amount to so many peripheral controlled zones. In any event, occasional rhetorical declamations to the contrary notwithstanding, they are scarcely anti-capitalist, offering no alternative to the 'modernisation' – *le dur commerce* – of whose contradictions and dislocations they are a symptom, rather than a solution. The dialectic of Enlightenment, so to speak, qualifies the Fukuyama thesis; it does not contradict it.

Another type of refutation disputed the uniformly liberal–capitalist reality of the OECD countries, underscoring the achievements of social democracy in regulating and humanising market mechanisms in Western Europe. These, it could be argued, were compounded by the continental tradition of Christian democracy, papal encyclicals subtending electoral cycles, to form the distinctive 'social model' that differentiates the European Union from US and Asian capitalisms. If so, no universal–homogeneous state could be posited as the end of history. In effect, this was tantamount to a form of discursive alchemy whereby, capitalism no longer being capitalism, it cannot be said to have triumphed. But Occam's razor turns against those who would wield it. A regulated capitalism – and what capitalism is not to some degree, other than in the neo-liberal utopia of those who desire its complete 'disembedding'? – remains capitalism, however ameliorated by welfare. Moreover, the 15 years since *The End of History and the Last Man* was published have witnessed an acceleration in the Americanisation of European social democracy, which has made its peace with the neo-liberal dispensation. For the likes of Schröder, Jospin, Prodi and Blair – *homo photo-opportunismus* – in power in the principal West

European states in the 1990s, there was no alternative to it, whatever the vapourings of the 'Third Way'. As for the suppositious counter-capitalist credentials of Wojtyla or Ratzinger, the record speaks – *urbi et orbi* – for itself.

A final line of resistance held out the converse consolation: namely, that formerly existing socialism was in no wise socialist; that its erasure from the geopolitical map could therefore not be taken as a 'world-historical' verdict on the possibility of a socialist alternative – indeed, the latter could only benefit from the termination of a travesty and tragedy in the East; and, consequently, that history could not be said to have ended in Fukuyaman terms. The conviction that the events of 1989–91 have not infirmed the Marxist theory of historical trajectory led Callinicos, for example, to object that there was a systemic alternative to liberal capitalism ignored, unsurprisingly, in Fukuyama's sense of an ending: revolutionary socialism.[64] But even were we to endorse his interpretation of the 'key empirical issue'; to accept that Stalinism was in fact 'a particular variant of capitalism' (i.e. 'bureaucratic state capitalism'); and thereby reconfigure the Cold War as one fought between competing capitalisms (liberal/state); and thus retrieve an unvanquished socialism from a Western capitalism victorious only over its Eastern alter ego – this would afford little or no consolation. For if the USSR and the Second World were not in any way socialist, then socialism has never existed. And if so, its viability as a systemic alternative to a seemingly indomitable capitalism remains undemonstrated – an inviolate ideal rather than a proven potential.[65]

Writing in *Le Monde* in October 1991, the Spanish ex-Communist Jorge Semprun suggested that 'today we are faced with this reality: the society in which we live is an untranscendable horizon'. His terms echoed a slogan with which the 1960s had opened – Sartre's celebrated characterisation of Marxism as 'the untranscendable philosophy of our time' – while revising its verdict.[66] Despite the arrival on the world scene of a spirited alter-globalisation movement a decade later, there are as yet no compelling reasons to overturn Semprun. On this score, the adventures of the dialectic to date have confirmed Fukuyama.

POSTFACE

Fifteen years on, and Fukuyama is keen to distance himself from various implications – alleged imputations – of his argument, drawn by friend and foe alike. How should we take his demurrers? As we have seen, with prudential caveats Fukuyama explicitly countenanced the use of force to align provinces still mired in history, if not for their own sake then for the security of the post-historical world: invoking classical authority, if you would have 'peace and prosperity', then prepare for war. The 'struggle for recognition' always logically extended beyond intra-societal to inter-state relations. For the originator of the concept, history might culminate in a rational hedonism, but the road to that end state was drenched with blood. Hegel had pronounced history a 'slaughter-bench'; Kojève, in what Vincent Descombes deems 'a terrorist conception of history', embroidered the conceit:

> '*Weltgeschichte ist Weltgericht*' ('World History is a tribunal that judges the World'). History is what judges men, their actions and opinions, and lastly their philosophical opinions as well. To be sure, History is, if you please, a long 'discussion' between men. But this *real* historical discussion is something quite different from a philosophic dialogue or discussion. The 'discussion' is carried out not with verbal arguments, but with clubs and swords or cannon on the one hand, and with sickles and hammers or machines on the other. If one wants to speak of a 'dialectical method' used by History, one must make clear that one is talking about methods of war and of work.[67]

The language needs updating; the point stands. The prefiguration of the victory of liberal principles in the French and American revolutions is sufficient evidence of the inexpungible role of violence in history. On Kojèvian premises, 'velvet' revolutions of the East European sort are an uncovenanted bonus. In the march towards a 'pacific union', the end of history could be expected, as it were, to repeat itself – the first time as comedy, the second time as force.

Fukuyama's subsequent disavowals, recapitulating an agonistic philosophy of history as a pacific theory of modernisation, eviscerate a distinctive thesis by stripping it of its 'primary motor'. Where erstwhile neo-conservative allies and others persevere, in a spirit of 'do not adjust your mindset – reality is at fault', Fukuyama would have his readers believe that *The End of History and the Last Man* was never 'a brief for American hegemony', let alone for 'coercive regime change'. Letter and spirit alike tell against any such straightforward innocence by dissociation.

Under a not nationally unspecific optical illusion, when 'looking around contemporary America' in 1992 Fukuyama had perceived no 'excess of *megalothymia*'.[68] This was quite simply because he was looking in the wrong place. The briefest glance at White House or Pentagon, Capitol Hill or Foggy Bottom, would have afforded an altogether different picture. Post-Cold War, collective *megalothymia* was alive and well – indeed, armed and extremely dangerous – as the messianic US 'exceptionalism', supercharged by Christian fundamentalism, that is extolled on an almost pan-partisan basis in the Land of the Free, and whose blessings could now be dispensed in more or less liberal doses to deserving, hitherto benighted sections of the human race. The 'spirit of 1776', Fukuyama claimed (foreshadowing Colin Powell's outlandish performance at the UN Security Council in the countdown to war in Iraq), had issued in a 'democratic revolution', which 'abolished the distinction between master and slave by making the former slaves their own masters'.[69] The US Constitution – a slaveholders' charter, the bicentenary of whose ratification fell, as if by miracle, in 1989 – was set alongside the Declaration of the Rights of Man and the Citizen as *fons et origo* of the now triumphant principles of liberty and equality.[70]

Cynics long ago remarked that the Pilgrim Fathers set sail for the New World less because they were being persecuted than because they were not allowed to persecute others. However that may be, coercive US intervention around the globe in pursuit of its manifest destiny has been a regular feature of its performance since it emerged as a great power. It has been conducted directly or by proxy, with or without a coalition of the complicit, and in a combination of Rooseveltian and Wilsonian modes (big stick, outsized Bible). Fukuyama remarked that his Universal History 'should imply ... the end of imperialism, and with it, a decrease in the likelihood of war based on imperialism'.[71] But that did not preclude either a vocation on the part of the USA to further the goal of Universal History, wherever possible, via a Pax Americana; or the maximum universalisation of US domestic arrangements as its optimal institutional embodiment. In any event, since the end of the Cold War the USA has unquestionably been *primus inter predatores*. At one point Fukuyama concedes that 'liberal democracies like the United States have at times acted like revolutionary ones as well, when it has sought to promote its form of government in unlikely places from Vietnam to Panama'.[72] The note of disapproval ('revolutionary') might be adduced as evidence for his dissent – in advance – from plans for 'coercive regime change'. Yet the value judgement is incompatible with even the superficial logic of his philosophy of history; while, excluding the temporal qualification ('at times'), the statement is unexceptionable as a rendition of the historical record, from Havana and Managua to Kabul and Baghdad.

Some three-quarters of a century ago, two precocious 'endists' teased their readers that with the Entente's victory in 1918, thanks to US men and *matériel*, 'America was ... clearly top nation and History came to a .'[73] Exactly what that ascendancy portends for a universal–homogeneous state of capitalist democracy beyond the ranks of today's OECD remains unfathomable. But post-historical patent pending, no obvious reversal of the cumulative verdicts handed down by the twentieth-century's 'immense wars of the spirit' – First, Second, Cold – is in the immediate offing. Meanwhile, Fukuyama's revision of his own history, prompted by the vicissitudes of the USA's war of spirit on 'terror' in the new millennium, permits a provisional conclusion. In view of the anti-communist context, it may take the form of a variation on an old East European theme: the future is uncertain; the past is unpredictable.

THREE

In Extremis: Eric Hobsbawm

Prefacing a new collection of his essays, *Globalisation, Democracy and Terrorism*, Eric Hobsbawm advises prospective readers that they 'supplement and bring up to date what I have written in earlier publications, notably ... *The Age of Extremes*, ... *The New Century* ... and *Nations and Nationalism*'[1] – to which we might add his 2002 autobiography, *Interesting Times*. All are replete with the kind of parenthetical laconic judgements – historical, political, intellectual, cultural – that are one of this writer's invariably pleasurable trademarks. Among the less happy instances of the latter, however, are some stray disparaging remarks Hobsbawm has directed at Fukuyama's 'end of history' thesis since 1990.[2] Redolent of a monologue of the deaf, as if he who listens is lost, their tenor conveys a recklessness about accuracy disconcerting in a historian (especially a great one). For Hobsbawm, Fukuyama is 'the Doctor Pangloss of the 1990s', therewith, presumably, meriting satirical treatment at the hands of a latter-day Voltaire. Hobsbawm's own fin-de-siècle verdict on the 'old century', returned in

Age of Extremes, was of course at the antipodes of the Panglossian outlook (mis)attributed to Fukuyama. That he has himself upheld it, in the light of intervening developments, in subsequent publications is reason enough for renewed attention to a text that has no obvious competitors (certainly not in English).

OBSERVATION AND PARTICIPATION

Published in 1994, *Age of Extremes* was widely received not only as Hobsbawm's 'masterpiece',[3] but as *a* masterpiece – the commanding historiographical synthesis on what it defines as the 'short twentieth century', from the outbreak of the First World War in 1914 to the dissolution of the Soviet Union in 1991. Within the generally favourable mainstream reception of it, two critical qualifications stood out. The first, familiar enough on such occasions, might be paraphrased thus: great book, shame about the Marxism – inviting the riposte that if *Age of Extremes* is the former, this is in some measure on account of the latter. The second was formulated by Tony Judt, scourge of communists and fellow-travellers of all stripes:

> If the virtues of this book derive from its engaged and personal quality, so do its defects – or rather its defect, for there is really only one, though it takes many forms. Because this is a story of Hobsbawm's own lifetime – a lifetime devoted since

youth ... to a single cause – he is understandably inclined to see the main outlines and conflicts of the era much as he saw them when they were unfolding. In particular, the categories right/left, fascist/Communist, progressive and reactionary seem to be very firmly set, and pretty much as they first presented themselves to Hobsbawm in the Thirties.[4]

In short, a seriously flawed book – marred not so much by the generally Marxist orientation as the specifically communist affiliations, consolidated in the 1930s, of its author, born in the year of the Bolshevik Revolution.

Whatever one makes of his estimate of the 'defect' he pinpoints, Judt identified the crux of the matter. Conjugating the two criticisms, we can illuminate some of the paradoxes of *Age of Extremes* by analysing the extent to which a certain Enlightenment Marxism supplies its architecture and shapes its argument at key points, as regards not only the results of historical communism, but also the prospects for contemporary capitalism. The upshot (to anticipate) is that Hobsbawm's history is neither as straightforwardly Marxist, nor as orthodoxly communist, as critics have maintained. Nor, for that matter, is it quite so anti-Fukuyaman, on an attentive reading of *The End of History and the Last Man* at least, as Hobsbawm himself supposes.

Hobsbawm was perfectly conscious of the problem raised by Judt. In the Preface to *Age of Extremes*, he underlines the difficulty facing him. Embarking on a history of the twentieth century will, he confides, be 'an autobiographical endeavour', in as much as he has 'accumulated views and prejudices about it as a contemporary rather than a scholar'; and not simply an observant contemporary, but a 'participant observer' (a member, indeed, of the Communist Party of Great Britain for more than half a century).[5]

Hobsbawm had entered that caveat before, in his marvellous 1973 collection *Revolutionaries*, when characterising himself as 'a Marxist of the "old left"', who has been 'a modest participant' in some of what he now surveys and 'a "participant observer"' of much of the rest of it.[6] Moreover, in an autobiographical sketch in the 1971 essay 'Intellectuals and Class Struggle', he evokes the 'milieu' he hailed from, providing one of the keys to a lifetime's observation and participation. It was, he writes,

> a milieu which is now virtually extinct, the Jewish middle-class culture of central Europe after the first world war ... [that] lived under the triple impact of the collapse of the bourgeois world in 1914, the October revolution and anti-semitism. ... What could young Jewish intellectuals have become under such circumstances? Not liberals of any kind, since the world of liberalism (which included social democracy) was precisely what had collapsed. ... We became either communists or

some equivalent form of revolutionary Marxists, or if we chose our own version of blood-and-soil nationalism, Zionists. But even the great bulk of young intellectual Zionists saw themselves as some sort of revolutionary Marxist nationalists. There was virtually no other choice. We did not make a commitment against bourgeois society and capitalism, since it patently seemed to be on its last legs. We simply chose *a* future rather than *no* future, which meant revolution. But it meant revolution not in a negative but in a positive sense: a new world rather than no world. The great October Revolution and Soviet Russia proved to us that such a new world was possible, perhaps that it was already functioning.[7]

It is the confounding of those expectations – the mingled hopes and fears of capitalist ashes and a socialist phoenix arising from them in the twentieth century – that Hobsbawm has to handle in *Age of Extremes*. In so doing, he faces a temptation, once again unerringly identified by him – this time in his reflections on the Bicentenary of the French Revolution, *Echoes of the Marseillaise*: 'All of us inevitably write out of the history of our own times when we look at the past and, to some extent, fight the battles of today in period costume.'[8]

As an initial minor symptom of the difficulty in the case to hand, we might note the very indeterminacy of the original title under which his book was published in the United Kingdom: not 'the age of extremes' – the definite article was prudently omitted and only added subsequently – but 'age of extremes'. For by what criterion could the short twentieth century be said to be *the* age of extremes? Then there is the category of 'extremism' itself. The titles of Hobsbawm's trilogy on the long nineteenth century, to which we shall turn in a moment, had been candidly Marxist: *The Age of Revolution*, *The Age of Capital*, *The Age of Empire*. Here, by contrast, we are in the presence of a category derived from the lexicon of a quotidian liberalism – not only the stock-in-trade of editorialising on, say, Islam ('moderates' versus 'extremists'); but (to move to a more elevated level) that of the 'end of ideology' theorists of the 1950s and 1960s – for example, Raymond Aron in *The Opium of the Intellectuals* in 1955, asserting (in terms which reappear in *Age of Extremes*) that 'the wars of secular religion are ending' or that 'Stalinism has been diffused in a century convulsed by catastrophes'.[9] (Part 1 of *Age of Extremes*, spanning 1914–45, is precisely entitled 'The Age of Catastrophe'.)

It is not that Hobsbawm, despite belated subscription to something like the 'end of ideology' thesis (itself the forerunner of the 'end of history' thesis), has straightforwardly embraced liberalism after all these years. Rather, the very idiom of his periodisation of the 'short twentieth century' attests to his enduring commitment to a particular variety of Enlightenment Marxism when interpreting the past and (albeit – or perhaps precisely because – now shorn of its progressivist optimism) prospecting the future. Doctrinal orthodoxy in the international communist movement from the mid 1930s, era of the anti-fascist Popular Frontism which 'continues to determine my strategic thinking in politics to this day',[10] that Marxism – as it were, Descartes, Voltaire, Marx, Stalin, *même combat*! – at once informs and deforms Hobsbawm's account of his century. Responding to François Furet's portrayal of the communist experience as a *passé plus qu'imparfait* in 1996, Hobsbawm remonstrated that it 'reads like a belated product of the Cold War', whereas 'any history of our times which hopes to survive into the next century must, after 1989, which clearly marks the end of an entire historic era, begin by trying to take a tentative step away from the ideological and political battlefields of that era'.[11] By the time of his autobiography six years later, as if half-conceding Judt's point, he was acknowledging that his own attempt at such a history 'was written with the passion that belongs to the age of extremes'.[12]

THE LONG NINETEENTH CENTURY

We may start with the past as prologue – Hobsbawm's trilogy on the 'long nineteenth century' of 1789–1914, which, in conjunction with *Age of Extremes*, offers a grand history of capitalist modernity. The trilogy was orthodoxly Marxist in both the titles of its instalments and its substance: in its overall conception of the historical period it treats. The governing principles, set out in the 'Overture' to *The Age of Empire* (1987), were threefold. First, the modern world had its origins in the 'dual revolution' of the late eighteenth century – the English industrial revolution and the French political revolution – which unleashed the 'great transformation': the transition to an unprecedented, specifically capitalist form of human society. Second, that transformation, driven by the contradictory dynamic of industrial capitalism, and its internal and external impacts on pre-capitalist social formations, had expanded out from its northern European birthplace to confront and conquer much of the globe in the nineteenth century. And third, modern world history was basically the history of the process of combined and uneven development triggered by a mode of production which, tendentially at any rate, was global. In Hobsbawm's words, '[e]ssentially the central axis round which I have tried to organize the history of the [long nineteenth] century is the triumph and transformation of capitalism in the historically specific forms of bourgeois society in its liberal version'. For the 'apogee' of 'bourgeois society in its liberal version' also sounded its death knell, as it fell 'victim [to] the very contradictions inherent in its advance': the 'strange death' of liberal capitalism and its civilisation in the second decade of the twentieth century.[13]

Yet an enterprise that might thereby appear to pertain to the historical genre of 'declinism' – e.g. Paul Kennedy's *The Rise and Fall of the Great Powers*

– while it does plot a 'rise and fall', does not depict it as an instance of some cyclical pattern to human history. For as had been made very clear at the inception of Hobsbawm's enterprise, notwithstanding the descent into barbarism on the eastern and western fronts of the First World War, capitalism potentially had an alternative – and superior – societal form ahead of it: the socialism for which, as Marx had all along insisted, it created the material and social preconditions.

In *The Age of Revolution*, published in 1962, Hobsbawm had argued that in the nineteenth century

> in a sense there was only one *Weltanschauung* of major significance and a number of other views which, whatever their merits, were at bottom chiefly negative critiques of it: the triumphant, rationalist, humanist 'Enlightenment' of the eighteenth century. Its champions believed firmly (and correctly) that human history was an ascent, rather than a decline or an undulating movement about a level trend. They could observe that man's scientific knowledge and technical control over nature increased daily. They believed that human society and individual man could be perfected by the application of reason, and were destined to be so perfected by history. On these points bourgeois liberals and revolutionary proletarian socialists were at one.[14]

Indeed, Marxism, as propounded in the *Communist Manifesto*, whose terminology Hobsbawm echoes in the following passage, was the legitimate inheritor of this Enlightenment progressivism:

> ... an ideology of progress implies one of evolution, possibly of inevitable evolution through stages of historical development. But it was not until Karl Marx ... transferred the centre of gravity of the argument for socialism from its rationality or desirability to its historic inevitability that socialism acquired its most formidable intellectual weapon, against which polemical defences are still being erected. ... capitalism could be shown by means of political economy to possess internal contradictions which inevitably made it at a certain point a bar to further progress and would plunge it into a crisis from which it could not emerge. Capitalism, moreover, ... inevitably created its own grave-diggers, the proletariat ... . As capitalism had prevailed, not simply because it was more rational than feudalism, but because of the social force of the bourgeoisie, so socialism would prevail because of the inevitable victory of the workers. It was foolish to suppose that it was an eternal ideal ... . It was the child of capitalism. It could not even have been formulated in an adequate manner before the transformation of society which created the conditions for it. But once the conditions were there, the victory was certain, for [in the words of Marx's 1859 Preface] 'mankind always sets itself only such tasks as it can solve'.[15]

It might be relevant – and is certainly only appropriate – to point out that this was written at the height of

Khrushchevite reformism in the Soviet Union, amid the euphoria induced by Soviet satellites and manned space flights. But even 25 years later – in the Conclusion to *The Age of Empire* – despite the much more sober tone, Hobsbawm, now writing during the Gorbachev interlude in the USSR and in the shadow of Chernobyl, was still striking a guardedly optimistic note about the prospects for the twenty-first century. For all that 'we can no longer believe that history guarantees us the right outcome, neither does it guarantee us the wrong one'. 'Is there', Hobsbawm mused, 'still room for the greatest of all hopes, that of creating a world in which free men and women, emancipated from fear and material need, will live the good life together in a good society?' His answer? A defiant question: 'Why not?'[16]

THE GATHERING GLOOM

Less than a decade later, painting it black, a very different picture is offered, encapsulated in the last word of *Age of Extremes* – 'darkness':

> We live in a world captured, uprooted and trans-
> formed by the titanic economic and techno-scientific
> process of the development of capitalism ... . We
> know, or at least it is reasonable to suppose, that
> it cannot go on *ad infinitum*. The future cannot be
> a continuation of the past, and there are signs ...

that we have reached a point of historic crisis. The forces generated by the techno-scientific economy are now great enough to destroy the environment, that is to say, the material foundations of human life. The structures of human societies themselves, including even some of the social foundations of the capitalist economy, are on the point of being destroyed by the erosion of what we have inherited from the human past. Our world risks both explosion and implosion. It must change.

… If humanity is to have a recognizable future, it cannot be by prolonging the past or present. If we try to build the third millennium on that basis, we shall fail. And the price of failure, that is to say, the alternative to a changed society, is darkness.[17]

Not only does history not ascend; not only does it not progress, if necessary (as Hegelian Marxists used to say) 'by the bad side'. What we are instead presented with is impending regression – as if, socialism having failed, Rosa Luxemburg's worst fears have been confirmed and the alternative to capitalism is set to be 'barbarism'. Indeed, in an article of that title published shortly before the release of *Age of Extremes*, Hobsbawm lamented 'the reversal of what we may call the project of the eighteenth-century Enlightenment, namely the establishment of a *universal* system of … rules and standards of moral behaviour, embodied in the institutions of states dedicated to the rational progress of humanity'.[18] What for Fukuyama was in the process of being realised, in however protracted and tortuous a fashion, courtesy of the elimination of liberalism's historic antagonist, was for Hobsbawm being negated, in large part because of the self-same cancellation of socialism in its communist incarnation. With the advent of one – neo-liberal – capitalist world, darkness, if it had yet to fall, had gathered.

What are we to make of this? According to Hobsbawm, *Age of Extremes* is structured as 'a sort of triptych':[19]

–   First, 'the age of catastrophe' from 1914 to 1945 – an era of two cataclysmic world wars, punctuated by the disastrous economic slump of the 1930s, volatilising political and economic liberalism and spawning Bolshevism and fascism.
–   Second, 'the golden age' from 1945 to circa 1973 – or the *trente glorieuses* of capitalism's unparalleled prosperity, transforming the globe more comprehensively and rapidly than at any time in human history; of communism's entrenchment in Eurasia, misfiring in its 'peaceful competition' with capitalism but spurring the latter to reform itself, seemingly for good – and certainly for the better; and of the Third World's hopeful inscription on the geopolitical map with decolonisation and the end of European empires.
–   Third, and finally, 'the landslide' of 1973–91 – or the relapse of global capitalist society into a chronic crisis of regulation even as it triumphed in the secular struggle with historical communism

which, ideologically at any rate, had held centre stage for four decades or more.

Contrary to Hobsbawm's unqualified ratification of it in *The Age of Revolution*, he now explicitly repudiated Marx's 'nineteenth-century optimism' that 'mankind always sets itself only such problems as it can solve'.[20] The interment of historical communism and resurgence of an irrational laissez-faire, laissez-aller witnessed, if not triggered, an extremity – the last extremity? – of historical capitalism.

Clearly, then, as Perry Anderson pointed out at the time of publication, the most striking feature of this periodisation is the 'reversal of verdicts' it operates.[21] For Hobsbawm, 1991 did not terminate the 'Evil Empire' and usher in a 'New World Order' of liberal–capitalist cornucopia. On the contrary, its 'consequences', deemed 'enormous and still not fully calculable', are adjudged to be 'mainly negative': 'the collapse of one part of the world revealed the malaise of the rest' – 'not a crisis of one form of organizing societies, but of all forms'.[22]

So much for the periodisation and overall evaluation of the short twentieth century. The composition of Hobsbawm's history corresponds, as Simon Bromley shrewdly noted in a review, to two rather different principles, which help explain its synthesis and table some of the relevant queries it invites, insofar as there is a latent tension between them.[23] The first, in conformity with the preceding nineteenth-century trilogy, is that of the development of an incipiently global capitalism in the twentieth century – a history whose *internal* dynamics Hobsbawm, declining recourse to the conceptual instruments of historical materialism, disclaims his ability adequately to explain. The second principle is new: that of the 'great contest' between capitalism and communism in the twentieth century – likewise a global history, with its matrix in the First World War (hence *Age of Extremes*' starting point in 1914 as opposed to 1917), and its terminus in Western victory in the Cold War (sealed in 1991). The point is this: in the absence of explanations of the internal dynamics of global capitalism – generating slump in the 1930s, boom in the 1950s and 1960s, stagflation in the 1970s, and so on – Hobsbawm resorts to accounting for much of its career in the short twentieth century by reference to the *external* dynamic set in motion by its systemic competition with communism.

Hence if the Russian Revolution was the bitter fruit of 1914, credit for liberal capitalism's unanticipated survival after its near-death experience in the 1930s and 1940s, and its mutation in the broadly Keynesian mould of the 'golden age' – 'a sort of marriage between economic liberalism and social democracy', in Hobsbawm's résumé[24] – can in the main be assigned to the record of the Soviet Union. Surveying it after the fall, historical communism has few intrinsic merits for Hobsbawm. Isolated in 'backward' agrarian zones, whose modernisation it effected or accelerated, it never represented a realistic alternative to advanced capitalism: 'the tragedy of the October Revolution was precisely that it could only produce its kind of ruthless, brutal, command socialism'.[25] '[F]ailure', he declares without further ado in *Interesting Times*, 'was built into this enterprise from the start'; 'as I now know, [it] was bound to fail'.[26] The game was effectively up with the abortion of the German – i.e. Western – revolution in 1918. Nevertheless, communism's 'direct and indirect effects' were momentous:

> Not least because it proved to be the saviour of liberal capitalism, both by enabling the West to win the Second World War against Hitler's Germany … and by providing the incentive for capitalism to reform itself and – paradoxically – through the Soviet Union's apparent immunity in the Great Depression, the incentive to abandon the belief in free market orthodoxy.[27]

Thus it is that the great cause of Hobsbawm's lifetime, deflated in its pretensions ever to have mounted a genuine societal challenge to advanced capitalism, is retrospectively exonerated via its indirect effects on, and unintended consequences for, capitalism. The USSR's victory in the Second World War salvaged and sparked a renaissance of liberalism; its sponsorship of 'planning' seeded the mechanisms of the 'golden age'; its 'threat' stimulated the post-war settlement; its sheer existence helped stabilise geopolitics, albeit in the glacis of the Cold War.

Consequently, Hobsbawm identifies the alliance against Nazism between Western liberal capitalism and Eastern communism as 'the hinge of the twentieth century and its decisive moment'.[28] This in turn permits him in the key fifth chapter, 'Against the Common Enemy', to vindicate the communism of the anti-fascist Popular Fronts and wartime Resistance. Here is what Francis Mulhern has defined as the 'moral centre of gravity' of Hobsbawm's account of the century:[29]

> ... as the 1930s advanced it became increasingly clear that more was at issue than the relative balance of power between the nation-states constituting the international ... system. Indeed, the politics of the West ... can best be understood, not through the contest of states, but as an international ideological civil war ... . And ... the crucial lines in this civil war were not drawn between capitalism as such and Communist social revolution, but between ideological families: on the one hand, the descendants of the eighteenth-century Enlightenment and the great revolutions, including, obviously, the Russian revolution; on the other, its opponents. In short, the frontier was not between capitalism and communism, but between what the nineteenth century would have called 'progress' and 'reaction'.[30]

This is the world Hobsbawm has lost: the universe of a communism aligned, in reality or rhetoric, with the best of liberalism in the cause of human progress; a time when *Internationale*, *Marseillaise* and *Star-*

Spangled Banner (if not *God Save the King*) could be intoned in unison; when English, American, French and Russian revolutions belonged to one and the same lineage; when a capacious syllabus of verities extended from Spartacus to Stalin. And while the collapse of communism, explicable in Marxian terms by the fettering of the productive forces by outmoded relations of production, and the disorientation of social democracy, attributable to the outflanking of nation-states by globalisation, do not rule out what Hobsbawm alludes to as 'the possibility of other kinds of socialism',[31] he now finds no firm grounds for a future socialism *internal* to capitalist societies. 'Socialism' predominantly figures in his analysis as an extra-capitalist force, in the shape of the Soviet Union and international communism.

From Hobsbawm's post-lapsarian perspective, with the ongoing trans-nationalisation of a heedless free-market capitalism the outlook is bleak. Humanity has posed itself problems – ecological, demographic, cultural, political, and so on – which, even where its guardians are cognisant of them, capitalism seemingly cannot solve. With the 'apparent failure of all programmes, old and new, for managing or improving the affairs of the human race',[32] the conclusion is inescapable and delivered in the 'bird's eye view of the century' with which *Age of Extremes* opens: 'the old century has not ended well'.[33]

NOT DARK YET

By way of response, there are two immediate ironies of history that need to be noted. The first concerns Hobsbawm's treatment of historical communism, in its temporary alliance, and prolonged contention, with liberal capitalism. In vaunting the coalition of 'progress' 'against the common enemy' of 'reaction' in Part 1, he glides over something he only addresses in Part 2 (in Chapter 8 on 'The Cold War') – namely, the Stalinist character of the communist party to the alliance, then at the pitch of *its* barbarism, as the great terror followed hard on the heels of forced collectivisation. Hobsbawm's amalgamation of liberal capitalism and communism into a single party of Enlightenment, casting Joe and Sam as avuncular affinities in a posthumous rehabilitation of Browderism, is sealed at the cost of repressing this: the degeneration of communism into a Stalinist barbarism, unredeemed by the thwarting of Barbarossa, which was decisive in tarnishing the image of socialism in the West (not to mention the East).

Second, it is surprising to find the Cold War – era of numerous sanguinary hot wars and other episodes of plentiful bloodletting in the Third World – featuring in Hobsbawm's 'Golden Age', on the basis that it provided a regulatory structure for the international system. With its termination, Hobsbawm writes, '[t]he Short Twentieth Century ended in problems, for which nobody had, or even claimed to have, solutions

... for the first time in two centuries, the world of the 1990s entirely lacked any international system or structure'.[34] Even were we to grant the substance of this claim, the obvious rejoinder is that with the 'solutions' on offer during the Cold War, humanity – and especially the 'damned of the earth' – had its fair share of problems.

The core issue, however, is Hobsbawm's treatment of liberal capitalism itself. The acute crisis of regulation and orientation afflicting what has become a global mode of production since the implosion of the Second World both allows him to qualify Western triumphalism post-1991 – Bush Senior's 'the Cold War is over and we won' – and to gesture at the continuing relevance of a social democratic version of socialism, thereby turning the tables on the likes of Fukuyama. In drawing – overdrawing – the contrast between the 'Golden Age' and the 'Landslide', Hobsbawm deploys a concept of economic crisis which, for better or worse, is not specifically Marxist. As Bromley has noted, it owes more to Polanyi's *The Great Transformation* – the depredations of disembedded markets – or Schumpeter's *Capitalism, Socialism and Democracy* – the self-destructive tendencies of untethered capitalism – than to Marx's *Capital*.[35] For unlike the 1930s depression, the crisis threatening the survival of capitalism and, with it, humanity on the eve of the third millennium is conceived by Hobsbawm in terms not of the internal contradictions of the capitalist mode of production, but of a chronic volatility consequent upon its transgression of its external limits. Consuming everything in its path, capitalism is self-consuming, as it erodes the non-capitalist sources of its own maintenance and reproduction: the Second World, the nation-state, the environment, community, family, morality, and so on. (Hence the tart disapproval, here and elsewhere, of the prevalent antinomianism unleashed by the 'cultural revolution' of the 1960s, on the part of an author who admits to possessing 'the instincts of a Tory communist, unlike the rebels and revolutionaries drawn to their cause by the dream of total freedom for the individual, a society without rules'.)[36] The erosion of non-market forces and resources of market regulation is construed as betokening a potentially terminal crisis of the self-*de*regulating and – if left to its own devices – ultimately suicidal global 'free market economy'.

The problem, in short, is that the sympathies of a lifetime's participant observation, together with Hobsbawm's own prior assimilation of the history of capitalism (contra Marx) to what Bromley neatly names the 'progress of reason',[37] induce a want of proportion in his closing assessment. In other words, they lead to Hobsbawm's equation of what, by the standards of post-war European social democracy, is a regression in human civilisation with a systemic crisis of liberal capitalism on a global scale, due to an absence of public intervention and regulation in defiance of what Hobsbawm in 1968 was confident enough to describe as 'the norm of history, and indeed of reason'.[38] Entering the lists against the 'dragon of unreason' (Freud), Hobsbawm's myopic rationalism prompts the thought that, had things gone as anticipated in *The Age of Revolution*, the final volume of his tetralogy would have been entitled nothing less than *The Age of Reason*, definite article and all.

We may now register a final irony. However seemingly divergent their conclusions and evaluations, the professedly Marxist Hobsbawm has something in common with the forthrightly anti-Marxist Fukuyama of the 1989 essay: namely, denial of any intrinsic contradictory logic to the capitalist mode of production – one of whose tendencies for Marx, as Hobsbawm had so rightly argued in *The Age of Revolution*, was the creation of a force internal to it, with the potential to challenge and redirect its logic: the 'collective labourer'. As we have seen, here, by contrast, socialism is enacted by a force external to capitalism: the formerly existing socialism of the Second World that galvanised formerly existing social democracy in the First.

Of course, there are reasonable grounds for Hobsbawm's pessimism of the intellect on this score. It can reasonably be argued that capitalism has dug the grave of the gravedigger nominated in the *Communist Manifesto*; and therewith interred the version of Enlightenment optimism about historical progress embodied, albeit in radicalised form, in classical Marxism and inherited by what Hobsbawm now demotes to the status of 'communist utopianism'.[39] Similarly, if his retrospective devaluation of the systemic competition between communism and capitalism as so much ideological sound and fury, signifying nothing, is scarcely convincing, his opinion that it was invariably an unequal contest, with only one likely victor, is compelling enough. But be that as it may, does it license Hobsbawm's main inference – namely, a dearth of any 'programmes ... for managing or improving the affairs of the human race', a lack of any prospective solutions to the world's problems, amid a crying absence of any international regulatory system or structure?

To pose the question is to prime the answer. Early on in his last chapter, Hobsbawm inquires: 'What ... were the international powers, old or new, at the end of the millennium?', and responds: 'The only state that would have been recognized as a great power, in the sense in which the word had been used in 1914, was the USA. What this meant in practice was quite obscure.'[40] Fleetingly glimpsed, one eminently discernible future is thereafter enshrouded in the gathering gloom. For in practice, what was meant by the existence and performance of the USA as the sole surviving 'great power' was not altogether obscure in 1994, even if it has become clearer thereafter. A nonplussed Hobsbawm cannot be reproached for failing to divine the precise contours of the US ascendancy commended in the 'Project for a New American Century'. Yet it is difficult to resist the conclusion that ideological antipathy has here got the better of historical sensibility, as if in the spirit of Freud's sometime confession of incomprehension:

'Yes, America is gigantic – a gigantic mistake.' After all, that imperial project unquestionably contains a programme for managing, and (so far as its protagonists are concerned at any rate) improving, the affairs of the human race – by promoting international capitalism in maximum accord with national interests and, to that end, striving for 'full spectrum dominance'. 'In the beginning all the world was America', Locke once famously wrote. In the unlikely event that the aspiring North American masters of the universe have their way, it (not to mention the Moon and Mars) will be in the end as well. Possibly for the first time, on this score the BBC World Service proved a surer guide to twenty-first century reality than a participant observer of much twentieth-century history, when in 2004 it broadcast a series devoted to the global role of the USA. Its title? What else? – 'The Age of Empire' (*with* the definite article).

AGE OF UNREASON?

Since 1994 Hobsbawm has brought the international role of the USA into somewhat sharper focus, noting in *The New Century* that it is 'the only country in history that has been in a position to claim world hegemony',[41] while evincing incredulity at the likelihood of its succeeding and expressing due dismay at the results of the endeavour. Castigating 'the sheer effrontery of presenting the establishment of a US global empire as the defensive reaction of a civilization about to be overrun by nameless barbarian hoards unless it destroys "international terrorism"', Hobsbawm writes in a powerful coda to *Interesting Times*:

> ... September 11 proved that we all live in a world with a single global hyperpower that has finally decided that, since the end of the USSR, there are no short-term limits on its strength and no limits on its willingness to use it, although the purposes of using it – except to manifest supremacy – are quite unclear. The twentieth century is over. The twenty-first opens on twilight and obscurity.[42]

The continuity with *Age of Extremes* – analytical, evaluative, even figurative – is patent. It is maintained in the lectures collected in *Globalisation, Democracy and Terrorism*, where the 'imperialism of human rights' is forthrightly rejected at the outset.[43] Hobsbawm proceeds to arraign a megalomaniacal US unilateralism, which ignores what (in an unwonted concession to the reigning hypocrisies) he at one point calls 'the international community',[44] as the greatest threat to world peace today. Will the United States, he asks, learn the lessons of his adopted country's realism about the limits of empire in the nineteenth and twentieth centuries? Or 'will it be tempted to maintain an eroding global position by relying on politico-military force, and in so doing promote not global order but disorder, not global peace but conflict, not the advance of civilization but of barbarism?'[45]

Inclined to suspect the latter, Hobsbawm exhibits disdain for 'the neo-conservative and neo-liberal utopians of a world of Western values spread by market growth and military interventions'.[46] Consternation at US squandering of the spoils of victory in the Cold War accompanies his scorn: 'The policies that have recently prevailed in Washington seem to all outsiders so mad that it is difficult to understand what is really intended.'[47] *All* outsiders? Unless (like Blair) they are honorary insiders, Berlusconi and Havel, not to mention Kouchner or Ignatieff – later cited by Hobsbawm as champions of B-52 humanitarianism[48] – would be surprised to hear it. More important than that rhetorical flourish is the imputation of insanity to US policy makers whom Hobsbawm twice dubs 'crazies',[49] in a terminology better suited to the saloon bar than the lecture theatre, and whose use suggests that the empire on which the sun never set has been erected into another 'norm of reason' (possibly even of history), this time imperial.[50]

Concluding his 1998 Introduction to the *Communist Manifesto*, Hobsbawm remarked that it is a

> document which envisaged failure. It hoped that the outcome of capitalist development would be a 'revolutionary reconstitution of society at large' but ... it did not exclude the alternative: 'common ruin'. Many years later, another Marxist rephrased this as the choice between socialism and barbarity. Which of these will prevail is a question which the twenty-first century must be left to answer.[51]

The original Marxian referent of that calamitous eventuality was not so much competing socio-economic systems, capitalist and socialist, as 'contending classes', bourgeoisie and proletariat.[52] But the point retains its relevance. And by now we have seen just how insistent Hobsbawm, taking counsel of his fears, has been on it across two decades: with the elimination of Soviet communism, the civilisation of (neo-)liberal capitalism is not *en rose* but *in extremis*. Yet this (as Perry Anderson has spotted) forms part of one of the 'two strategies of consolation'[53] engaged in by Hobsbawm when contemplating the common ruin of the fraternal enemies that were once communism and social democracy. Neither strategy, Anderson persuasively argues, warrants assent. Where the notion of a congress of the Enlightenment victors post-1989 was always utterly implausible, comfort for Candides, woe to the victors and vanquished alike is scarcely less so. If in the guise of its antonym, the cunning of reason – more Hegel than Voltaire – may yet end up having the last word.

FOUR

Ringing Out the Old: Perry Anderson

In *Considerations on Western Marxism*, released in 1976, Perry Anderson broadcast an affiliation to the Trotskyist tradition long evident from the pages of *New Left Review* under his editorship.[1] Among its defining characteristics, in its orthodox forms, was a historico-political perspective that regarded the Soviet Union (and cognate regimes in the Second World) as 'workers' states' – if not socialist, then certainly post-capitalist social formations, whose complexly contradictory character dictated rejection of Stalinism and anti-Sovietism alike. In Anderson's case, this orientation received a Deutscherite inflection. Soviet power, hybrid at home (abolition of private ownership of the means of production/imposition of bureaucratic dictatorship on the proletariat), was a comparable admixture abroad, by turns reactionary (Hungary, Czechoslovakia) and progressive (Cuba, Vietnam, Angola). The possible regeneration of the Russian Revolution, whether by way of proletarian revolution from below (Trotsky), or élite reformation from above (Deutscher), remained an article of faith among Marxists of this observance to the end. Most significantly of all, whatever its subsequent fate, October 1917 was said by Anderson in *Arguments Within English Marxism* (1980) to have set in train an 'irreversible ... alteration of the potential of historical action, in the course of the 20th century'.[2]

CORSI E RICORSI

No better summary of the implications of Anderson's outlook is to be had than a commentary by him, dating from 1983, on the relationship between Western Marxism and historical communism:

> The Western Marxist tradition had always been marked by a peculiar combination of tension and dependence in its relation to it. On the one hand, this was a filiation which from its very outset ... had embodied hopes and aspirations for a developed socialist *democracy* which the implacable machinery of bureaucratic dictatorship crushed in the USSR with the rise of Stalin. However mediated, sublimated or displaced ... the ideal of a political order beyond capital that would be more, rather than less, advanced than the parliamentary regimes of the West, never deserted it. Hence the permanently critical distance of the Western Marxist tradition from the state structures of the Soviet Union. ... On the other hand, this tradition nearly always had a

sense of the extent to which the Russian Revolution and its sequels, whatever their barbarities or deformities, represented the sole real breach with the order of capital that the twentieth century has yet seen – hence the ferocity of the onslaughts of the capitalist states against them. ... In the West, moreover, the alternative tradition within the labour movement, that of social-democracy, had lost any force of real opposition to capitalism, becoming a generally servile prop of the status quo. There, the only militant adversaries the local bourgeoisies encountered continued to be Communist Parties ideologically bound to the USSR.[3]

In print in English, Anderson kept his own counsel on the chances of the Soviet reform being steered (if, in retrospect, that is quite the right word) by Gorbachev. However, in correspondence with Norberto Bobbio published in Italian, he cautiously entertained 'the prospect for a liberal socialism in the post-revolutionary societies':

Of course, the outcome ... could not be less certain. *Perestroika* could miss a liberal socialism from either end, so to speak – that is, collapse back into the previous dictatorial regime, or flee forward into a de facto recreation of capitalism; possibly even combine these evils. But to use your terms, a liberal socialism must now be reckoned – in the medium to long run – as one not unrealistic historical possibility, among others, in the USSR. ...

> But if this is the case, the difference between our
> positions narrows greatly. ... a liberal socialism would
> be the common aim ... reached by the *corsi e ricorsi*
> of a staggeringly illiberal historical process.[4]

Once the hopes invested in that (warily formulated)
'not unrealistic historical possibility' had been dashed,
with the visiting of the second of the 'evils' envisaged
by Anderson – 'a de facto recreation of capitalism' in
the East – what was to be said (and done)?

An initial answer was forthcoming in 'The Ends
of History', published in 1992. Reconstructing the
genealogy of a notion recently resuscitated by Fukuyama,
inspecting the credentials of his rendition of it, and
arbitrating between the author and his critics, Anderson
extracted the rational kernel of the thesis and regretfully
endorsed it as a judgement on historical socialism
(communism and social democracy).[5] By 1998, in a
further unanticipated move, given Anderson's previous
censure of postmodernism in its Lyotardian incarnation,[6]
a *nihil obstat* to the discourse of postmodernity was
being issued to Fredric Jameson's capture of it 'for the
cause of a revolutionary Left'.[7] Postmodernism did
after all constitute 'the cultural logic of a capitalism'
which, while it would be rash to call it 'late' (for
what?), was unquestionably 'complacent beyond
precedent'.[8] On Anderson's mapping, the political
coordinates of its emergence consisted in the very
conjuncture that permitted Fukuyama's promulgation
of the 'end of history':

By the end of the [1980s], the post-war mission of social-democracy in Western Europe – a welfare state based on full employment and universal provision – had been largely abandoned by the Socialist International. In Eastern Europe and the Soviet Union, Communism – unable to compete economically abroad or democratise politically at home – was obliterated altogether. In the Third World, states born from national liberation movements were everywhere trapped in new forms of international subordination. ...

The universal triumph of capital signifies more than just a defeat for all those forces once arrayed against it, although it is also that. Its deeper sense lies in the cancellation of political alternatives.[9]

Underlying such conclusions was not simply observation of the dénouement of historical socialism, but tacit recognition that the Archimedean *terra firma* for changing the world staked out by the *Communist Manifesto*, and occupied by its inheritors thereafter, had been undermined. With its ongoing profound recomposition, the working class was not primed to play the part of capitalist gravedigger allocated it in the classical scripts and stoutly defended by Anderson in *In the Tracks of Historical Materialism* (as well as by colleagues in *New Left Review*), during the revisionist controversy of the early 1980s triggered by Eric Hobsbawm's 1978 Marx Memorial Lecture, 'The Forward March of Labour Halted?'. Accordingly, perhaps it was – or should have been – the less surprising when, on millennial cue, a second series of the *Review* was launched in January 2000, with an arresting 20-page editorial by Anderson enjoining a new course: 'Renewals'.

THE REFOUNDING MOMENT

Anderson conducted his reorientation of *New Left Review* by means of a comparison and contrast between its 'founding moment' in the post-1956 conjuncture in world politics and a refounding moment: the new global conjuncture – or would it turn out to be an epoch? – ushered in by the seismic events of 1989–91. He did so under three rubrics – the political, the intellectual and the cultural – which I shall follow here, albeit assigning greatest weight to the first.

Geopolitically, the founding moment had been defined by the de facto existence of three worlds: the First World of advanced capitalism, then booming; the Second World of backward socialism, finally reforming; and a Third World including nations that had wrested independence from their colonial masters or were struggling for it. Despite the more or less complete incorporation of European social democracy into the administration of welfare capitalism, socialism remained a spectre haunting the First World:

> Politically, a third of the planet had broken with capitalism. Few had any doubts about the enormities

of Stalin's rule, or the lack of democracy in any of
the countries that described themselves as socialist.
But the Communist bloc ... was still a dynamic
reality. ... Khrushchev ... held out promise of reform
in the USSR. The prestige of Maoist China was
largely intact. The Cuban Revolution was a new
beacon in Latin America. The Vietnamese were
successfully fighting the United States in South-East
Asia. Capitalism, however stable and prosperous in
its Northern heartlands, was – and felt itself to be
– under threat across the larger part of the world
outside them. Even at home, in Western Europe
and Japan, mass Communist movements were still
ranged against the existing order.[10]

Intellectually, the desacralisation of Stalin and
relaxation of Cold War orthodoxies prompted the
recovery or discovery of alternative Marxisms linked
to political practice – Trotskyism, Luxemburgism,
Maoism, Council communism, and so on – as well
as the assimilation of the various national theoretical
traditions – French (Sartre and Althusser), German
(Adorno and Marcuse), Italian (Della Volpe and
Colletti) – in a still highly productive Western Marxism.
These were flanked by French structuralism – Barthes,
Lévi-Strauss and co. – at the time commonly identified
with the left. In culture more generally, an equally
'abrupt rupture' with the stifling conformism of the
1950s could be identified in the emergence of rock
music and *auteur* cinema.[11]

Forty years on, what survived of this political–intellectual–cultural landscape? In sum, precious little. The

Second World had been obliterated and the Third World tamed. Socialism had disappeared from respectable political discourse and Marxism eclipsed as a term of intellectual reference. The collapse of the Soviet bloc had set in train a process issuing in 'the virtually uncontested consolidation, and universal diffusion, of neo-liberalism' by the century's end:[12] the defining characteristic of the refounding moment.

Six interrelated developments underlay or complemented the irresistible rise of neo-liberalism.

First, the reassertion of US prepotency across the board – economically, politically, culturally and militarily – confounding those who had wagered on the prospects of East Asian or Rhenish models of capitalism in the aftermath of the Cold War.

Second, the implementation of neo-liberal policy prescriptions by social democratic governments throughout Europe in the late 1990s, discomfiting expectations that the reformist tradition of the Second International would come into its own once untainted by guilt by association with communism.

Third, the termination of the Japanese economic miracle and the more or less voluntary servitude of Asia's (and the world's) most populous states – China and India – to the (de)regulatory bodies of the Washington consensus.

Fourth, the reduction of Russia's economy under 'shock therapy' to a chronic condition, rendering its pliable oligarchy ever more dependent on Western grace and favour.

Fifth, a decisive ideologico-political development capping these socio-economic changes – the confection of Clinton and Blair's 'Third Way' as a neo-liberalism with a human face, consummating the triumph of free-market capitalism by proving not merely in words but in deeds that there was no genuine alternative to it on offer:

> Ideologically, the neo-liberal consensus has found a new point of stabilization in the 'Third Way' of the Clinton–Blair regimes. The winning formula to seal the victory of the market is not to attack, but to preserve, the placebo of a compassionate public authority, extolling the compatibility of competition with solidarity. The hard core of government policies remains further pursuit of the Reagan–Thatcher legacy, on occasion with measures their predecessors did not dare enact. ... But it is now carefully surrounded with subsidiary concessions and softer rhetoric. The effect of this combination, currently being diffused throughout Europe, is to suppress the conflictual potential of the pioneering regimes of the radical right, and kill off opposition to neo-liberal hegemony more completely. ... For the quietus to European social-democracy or the memory of the New Deal to be consummated, governments of the Centre-Left were indispensable. In this sense, adapting Lenin's maxim that 'the democratic republic is the ideal political shell of capitalism', we could say that the Third Way is the best ideological shell of neo-liberalism today.[13]

The sixth and final shift was military and diplomatic: the demonstration war in the Balkans waged by NATO without UN sanction, setting a precedent for further such ventures in armed 'humanitarian' interventionism.

How had opponents responded? 'If we look at the spectrum of what was the traditional – formerly socialist – Left, two types of reaction to the new conjuncture predominate', so Anderson reckoned. The first took the form of 'accommodation' – coming to terms with the new dispensation on its terms (in the manner of Anthony Giddens's *The Third Way*); the second resorted to 'consolation' – refusing to concede while conjuring up new mornings or divining 'silver linings' (Eric Hobsbawm's *Age of Extremes* would be taken to task by Anderson on this score in 2002).[14] A pregnant footnote nuanced so stark a polarity:

> It is a matter of logic that there is a third possible reaction to the turn of the time, that is neither accommodation nor consolation: namely, resignation – in other words, a lucid recognition of the nature and triumph of the system, without either adaptation or self-deception, but also without any belief in the chance of an alternative to it. A bitter conclusion of this kind is, however, rarely articulated as a public position.[15]

Relegated to the foot of the page, these lines may be regarded as supplying the key to Anderson's own position, with two major qualifications: albeit hinted at, it was not publicly articulated as such; and after 'without any belief in the chance of an alternative to it', we should probably insert 'for the foreseeable future'. We shall return to this. For now, we may note that, distinguishing between the respective duties of a political movement and an intellectual journal, Anderson commended a stance of 'uncompromising realism' in the case of the latter – 'uncompromising in both senses', he stipulated: 'refusing any accommodation with the ruling system, and rejecting every piety and euphemism that would understate its power'.[16]

Putative counter-trends – the diffusion of democracy, advances in women's emancipation, increasing awareness of ecological perils – proved on inspection to be something less than counter-weights:

> The spread of democracy as a substitute for socialism, as hope or claim, is mocked by the hollowing of democracy itself in its capitalist homelands, not to speak of its post-communist adjuncts: steadily falling rates of electoral participation, increasing financial corruption, deadening mediatization. In general, what is strong is not democratic aspiration from below, but the asphyxiation of public debate and political difference by capital above. The force of this order lies not in repression, but dilution and neutralization; and so far, it has handled its newer challenges with equanimity. The gains made by the feminist and ecological movements in the advanced world are real and welcome: the most important elements of human progress in these societies in the last thirty years. But to date

they have proved compatible with the routines of accumulation. Logically, a good measure of political normalization has followed.[17]

Ideologically, the power of the new order was quite simply awesome:

> The novelty of the present situation stands out in historical view. It can be put like this. For the first time since the Reformation, there are no longer any significant oppositions – that is, systematic rival outlooks – within the thought-world of the West; and scarcely any on a world scale either, if we discount religious doctrines as largely inoperative archaisms .... Whatever limitations persist to its practice, neo-liberalism as a set of principles rules undivided across the globe: the most successful ideology in world history.[18]

With the advent of a now dominant postmodernism and wholesale commodification of erstwhile counter-cultures; with the monuments of revolutionary and reformist socialism alike consigned, like so many ichthyosauri, to the intellectual equivalent of the Natural History Museum; with the ventilation throughout the Anglophone academy of 'post-Marxist' paradigms vitiated by 'obscurantism' and 'populism' ('or – still worse – a mixture of the two, parading a weird blend of the demagogic and apolitical'[19]); and with the inverse ratio between academy and polity, such that the commanding heights were held by thinkers of the right – Fukuyama, Huntington, Yergin, Friedman et al. – capable of addressing a 'broad international public' impervious to the hermetic idioms of the progressive professoriate;[20] in these circumstances, the left, if not without intellectual resources (Hobsbawm and Jameson, Brenner and Arrighi, Eagleton and Harvey, etc.), had to confront a 'radical discontinuity' in its culture.[21]

The traditional centrality to that culture of the working class was rescinded by omission. Today 'everywhere on the defensive', organised labour's intra-modal ability to resist capital, let alone its inter-modal capacity to supplant it, had been put to the question, exposing more of its limitations than its possibilities as a self-emancipatory social agent. The upshot was unequivocal:

> The only starting-point for a realistic Left today is a lucid registration of historical defeat. Capital has comprehensively beaten back all threats to its rule, the bases of whose power – above all, the pressures of competition – were persistently under-estimated by the socialist movement. ...
>
> For the Left, the lesson of the past century is one taught by Marx. Its first task is to attend to the actual development of capitalism ... No collective agency able to match the power of capital is yet on the horizon. ... But if the human energies for a change of system are released again, it will be from within the metabolism of capitalism itself. ... Only in the evolution of this order could lie the secrets of another one.[22]

As to the divination of those secrets, Anderson conjectured that

> [i]t is unlikely the balance of intellectual advantage will alter greatly before there is a change in the political correlation of forces, which will probably remain stable so long as there is no deep economic crisis in the West. Little short of a slump of inter-war proportions looks capable of shaking the parameters of the current consensus. But that is no reason to mark time – polemic or analytical – in the interim.[23]

Setting aside the precise polemical and analytical editorial agenda submitted by Anderson, as well as the implementation (or non-implementation) of it in the pages of *New Left Review* thereafter, we may conclude our exposition of 'Renewals' by noting the classically Marxist order of determination proposed in the above passage, proceeding as it does from the economic ('deep economic crisis'), via the political ('the correlation of political forces'), to the ideological ('the balance of intellectual advantage').

GRIEF IN THE ZEITGEIST?

In one of the letters included in *The Postmodern Explained to Children*, Jean-François Lyotard mused that '[t]here is a sort of grief in the *Zeitgeist*. It can find expression in reactive, even reactionary, attitudes or in utopias – but not in a positive orientation which would open up a new perspective.'[24] Immune to such timely meditations when first broadcast, was Anderson succumbing to their seductions 15 years later?

To varying degrees, a host of left-wing commentators on his stocktaking thought so, charging him with 'defeatism' and 'pessimism'. One – the Russian Marxist, Boris Kagarlitsky – went so far as to speak of 'the suicide of *New Left Review*', in an overwrought response that was no advertisement for the analytical purchase of the revolutionary Marxism professed by its author.[25] What particularly rankled with critics was that Anderson's 'results and prospects' appeared hard on the heels of the irruption of the 'anti-globalisation' movement at Seattle, which supposedly signalled that the neo-liberal tide had turned, therewith infirming his master thesis. This, so it was felt, rendered his habitually Olympian perspective positively intergalactic and his posture of reality instructor irksome. Against such a backdrop, insistence that the 'first commitment [of] an intellectual journal must be to an accurate description of the world, no matter what its bearing on morale may be',[26] was widely received as a gratuitous provocation, slighting the anti-capitalist potential of popular mobilisations in the present. Persistently questioned about Seattle at a conference in New York state in October 2000, Anderson reportedly answered by recourse to an English proverb: 'there's a danger of taking one swallow for a summer'.[27]

A more balanced rejoinder to 'Renewals' came from the French Trotskyist Gilbert Achcar. He took issue with the 'crude economic determinism' on display in the passage from 'Renewals' quoted above, arguing that Anderson's historical sense deserted him when, in an aberrant wagering on the worse, he looked to 'a slump of inter-war proportions' to redound to the benefit of the left. On the other hand, Achcar noticed something of a paradox missed by many others: 'In reality, Perry Anderson's editorial expresses profound pessimism while simultaneously and unmistakably marking a new radicalization: the editor of *NLR* displays a particularly combative mood.'[28] This qualified, without altogether cancelling, what was deemed to be Anderson's 'historical pessimism' – the stance of someone 'who has more and more become a practitioner of the "pessimism of the intellect" championed by Gramsci'.[29]

Champion of Gramsci though he undoubtedly is, Anderson would nevertheless dissent here, declining to subscribe to the Sardinian's voluntaristic couplet: 'pessimism of the intellect, optimism of the will'. As we have seen, the posture he commends is one of 'uncompromising realism', repudiating the option of pessimism or optimism, whether of the intellect or the will, as fallacious. At one point in *The Origins of Postmodernity*, Anderson notes the

deeply Hegelian cast of [Jameson's] Marxism, which has equipped him to confront the adversities of the epoch, and work through its confusions, with an intrepid equanimity all his own. Categories such as optimism or pessimism have no place in Hegel's thought. Jameson's work cannot be described as optimistic, in the sense in which we can say of the Western Marxist tradition that it was pessimist. Its politics have always been realist.[30]

Predicated of Jameson, these propositions (minus the 'deeply Hegelian cast') are equally applicable to Anderson's Marxism. The analytical duty to be discharged, closer in temper to Spinoza's *non ridere, non lugere neque detestari, sed intelligere* (not to ridicule, not to lament or execrate, but to understand) than to Gramsci's 'pessimism of the intellect', is accurate reflection of the state of the world. But that need not preclude resistance to it.

Two key questions, then: did 'Renewals' broadly reflect the trends of contemporary political history at the time it was written? And has the reaction of 'resignation' – even with the qualification: 'for the foreseeable future' – precluded resistance to them?

Given the Deutscherite cast of Anderson's Marxism over more than four decades, it would have been surprising to find him enjoining anything other than 'a lucid registration of historical defeat' as the sole plausible starting point for what was left of the traditional left in 2000. Such a conclusion followed with impeccable logic from Andersonian premises. However, consistency is one thing; cogency, another. On the latter count,

Anderson could quite legitimately maintain that the left's current situation was stamped by two undeniable, correlated realities. The first was the global crisis of socialism, in the shape of the regimes, movements and intellectual systems historically associated with it. Both the principal traditions of socialism in the twentieth century had expired towards its close, with the implosion of communism and abdication of social democracy. Notwithstanding the manifold vices of the Second World, founded in a break with capitalism it had thereafter operated as an objective counter to imperialism. Consequently, its erasure from the geopolitical map constituted a signal victory for the First World and crucial defeat for the Third World, massively constraining the room for manoeuvre in the South. Even in the North itself, the communist parties descended from the Third International had, for all their demerits, at least functioned as an 'institutionalized reminder, [a] mnemonic device ... holding the place [of socialism] in the pages of history'.[31]

In the wake of 1989, it had of course been suggested that the beneficiary would be the other main tradition in socialist politics – the social democracy of the Second International. In the event, as Anderson argued, the reverse was the case. In the inter-war period, social democracy pursued an unavailing reformist road to socialism. In the post-war period, it effectively retracted the goal of socialism for the regulation and humanisation of capitalism. Since the crisis of the Keynesian settlement in the 1970s, it has largely renounced reformism in the second (post-war) sense and gravitated to a more emollient – social–liberal – version of the neo-liberal consensus. The turning point came in southern Europe in the early 1980s, when the French Socialist Party, elected on a manifesto that promised Rimbaud (*Changer la vie*), delivered Rocard (demonstrating the truth of Jean Jaurès's acid remark that you can get anywhere in socialism, as long as you get out of it). This was clearly attested in the late 1990s, with the election of social democratic governments across the European Union. Repudiating the very idea of a second way, under the shelter of the third they fast-tracked to the first: *via dollarosa*. As *The Times* noted with satisfaction, the forced resignation in 1999 of German Finance Minister Oscar Lafontaine – a Euro-Keynesian – was, in its bathetic way, as significant an event in the history of social democracy as the demolition of the Berlin Wall a decade earlier had been in the history of communism. Ending less with a bang than a whimper, social democracy signed the instrument of surrender presented it by neo-liberalism.

With the conclusion of the 'great contest' – and this was the second incontrovertible fact – the winning Cold War formula of neo-liberalism sponsored by Thatcher and Reagan in the 1980s had become the dominant ideology and policy of a now globally unchecked free-market capitalism under US intendancy. Capitalism is not proof against the economic distempers or social discontents provoked by its competitive logic, any more than US hegemony is untrammelled across five continents: ascendancy is not invincibility. Yet for all its actual or potential disorders, a New World Order has indeed been constructed on the ruins of formerly existing socialism and nationalism.

Granted, critics might riposte. But even if Anderson was right about the conjuncture of the first half of the 1990s – the depletion of First World social democracy, Second World communism and Third World nationalism as alternatives to free-market capitalism – had he not overlooked the impending doom of neo-liberalism spelt by the East Asian financial crisis of 1998, and depreciated the gathering forces of resistance to it? A decade on, it would seem clear that recurrent reports of neo-liberalism's demise, like those of Mark Twain's death, have been so many exaggerations, taking the wish for the reality. As for the culture of resistance to the New World Order, it was in its infancy in 1999: one swallow did not indeed make a summer. Alternatively put, contemporary hyperbole to the contrary notwithstanding, unlike ten days in Petrograd, five days in Seattle did not shake the world. A sense of proportion is indicated. Even today, the resilient 'movement of movements' against neo-liberalism, surviving concerted efforts to tar it with the brush of fundamentalism and terrorism, is a long way short of achieving the social weight and political focus, let alone institutional representation, required to table a systemic alternative to capitalism, of the sort once embodied in the mass organisations, political and trade union, of the Second and Third Internationals, which mobilised big battalions against the 'artillery of commodities'. The cruces of an alternative – agency, organisation, strategy, goal – that could command the loyalties and energies of the requisite untold millions await anything approaching resolution.

REFLECTION AND RESISTANCE

If it seems difficult to gainsay the thrust of Anderson's overview from – and for – the left, then it represented not a transcription of political pessimism, still less a gesture of intellectual suicide, but a historical realism reflecting the current supremacy of capitalism and its culture on a world scale, while canvassing, in its own distinctive fashion, resistance to it. That this is so is evident from Anderson's subsequent publications, clarifying his trajectory in the new century, where the 'radicalization' and 'combative mood' described by Achcar are plain for all to see. The most substantial of them to date is *Spectrum* (2005), a collection of articles on conservative, liberal and socialist intellectuals, panning from Schmitt and Hayek across Rawls and Habermas to Thompson and Timpanaro, which confirms Anderson's status as the finest socialist essayist of his generation. Unwavering in its political commitments, it is correspondingly astringent in its judgements (incidentally, exemplifying the author's disarming habit of proffering bouquets before delivering brickbats). Flanking it is a series of more directly political writings – among them, editorials on the 2000 US presidential election, the Palestinian question and internationalism; country studies of Germany, Italy, Brazil, France and Russia; and interventions, in the wake of al-Qaeda's attack on the World Trade Center, dealing with 9/11, the anti-war movement, and the 'new world hegemony'. (A collection of these, *Extra Time: World Politics since 1989*, containing 'a conclusion [that] reviews the condition of the left in the contemporary world', was announced by Verso in 2003 but has yet to appear.)

Their tenor, and the moral consistently pointed by Anderson, can be conveyed by a single brief quotation from a *New Left Review* editorial on US hegemony: 'The arrogance of the "international community" and its rights of intervention across the globe are not a series of arbitrary events or disconnected episodes. They compose a system, which needs to be fought with a coherence not less than its own.'[32] That system, with its contemptible train of hypocrisies and pieties, has been targeted with unremitting hostility by Anderson since 2001 – albeit, on occasion, in ways unconducive to fashioning a political strategy for opposing it. Thus, to take a widely noticed piece written during the run-up to the invasion of Iraq, and published a few weeks after mammoth anti-war demonstrations across the world, Anderson's seemingly symmetrical treatment of supporters and opponents led some to infer – wrongly – that he was wishing a plague on both houses. As its title ('Casuistries of peace and war') indicated, although conceding that '[g]reat mass movements are not to be judged by tight logical standards', much of the article was in fact taken up with uncovering 'a set of common assumptions' – about the United Nations and the 'international community', national sovereignty and humanitarian intervention, 'weapons of mass destruction' and Iraqi culpability – as if the most pressing task of the hour was to offer the burgeoning anti-war movement lessons in logic. In the conviction that '[r]esistance to the ruling dispensation that can last has to find another, principled basis', Anderson drafted a 'different set of premises': the 'international community' as 'a euphemism for American hegemony'; the UN Security Council as a cipher for the same; the Non-Proliferation Treaty as a mechanism for preserving nuclear oligopoly; the threat of 'international terrorism' as an imposture; the myth of a uniquely iniquitous Iraq; flagrant partiality over transgressions of national sovereignty, violations of human rights, and interdictions of 'weapons of mass destruction'. These, for all that they were persuasive in themselves, would more constructively have formed Anderson's main subject, rather than a vituperative pendant to it.[33]

In this regard, a paper on 'La batalla de ideas en la construcción de alternativas' delivered in Havana in August 2003 seems more attuned to the dual desiderata of stimulating reflection *and* stirring up resistance. Beginning with a sketch of the post-Cold War 'new world hegemony' – naming the system, as it were – Anderson proceeded to an exploration of the geographical zones of opposition to it, fixing on Latin America as the most promising terrain for a 'broad front of resistance' encompassing movements and governments. Criticism of 'key concepts' of the 'resistance front' was not muted, as Anderson set about puncturing illusions in the UN and (possibly disinhibited by his surroundings) cautioning against the ubiquitous inflation of 'human rights', incense on stilts where not 'honey on a sharp knife' (to borrow a Tibetan expression).[34] But the reader has more sense of engagement with – rather than instruction to – an audience.

Concluding his account of Jameson's work, Anderson observed:

> It is the complete extinction of the Communist alternative, its virtual deletion from the historical record, followed by the relentless advance of neo-liberalism through the Third World ... that forms the background to Jameson's now more uncompromising tone. ... Jameson's voice has been without equal in the clarity and eloquence of its resistance to the direction of the time. When the Left was more numerous and confident, his theoretical world kept a certain distance from immediate events. As the Left has become increasingly isolated and beleaguered, and less capable of imagining any alternative to the existing social order, Jameson has spoken ever more directly to the political character of the age ... .[35]

Excluding the flourish about Jameson as nonpareil, no more apt characterisation of Anderson's own recent work, in its conjoint reflection of, and resistance to, the 'direction of the time', could be penned. Prefacing *English Questions* in 1992, he had held up to his readers 'the example set by Gramsci': 'In the depths of his own defeat, Gramsci's strength of mind was to bring moral resistance and political innovation together. In related circumstances, this is the combination needed today.'[36] A decade later, Anderson drew the 'more general lesson' afforded by Hobsbawm's cushioning of his defeat by resort to dubious compensations in *Age of Extremes*: 'Accurate intelligence of the enemy is worth more than bulletins to boost doubtful morale. A resistance that dispenses with consolations is always stronger than one that relies on them.'[37] Dispensing with consolations in his calibration of the balance of forces, combining realism of the intellect and intransigence of the will, Perry Anderson has rung out the old in convincing fashion – a necessary condition, if alas an insufficient one, for any subsequent ringing in of the new.

Conclusion: Starting Over?

With the deletion of communism in the Second World, sanitisation of social democracy in the First and exhaustion of nationalism in the Third – in sum, with the remorseless capitalist standardisation of political culture across the globe – Fukuyama proclaimed the end of history, Hobsbawm feared a descent into darkness, and Anderson announced an utterly unprecedented neo-liberal ascendancy.

No sooner was the (virtual) ink dry on the draft of Anderson's balance sheet than a spectre, replacing the one brandished in the *Communist Manifesto* 150 years earlier, loomed up to haunt the World Trade Organisation and International Monetary Fund – what respectable opinion likes to demean as the 'anti-globalisation movement' (with its connotations of protectionism, chauvinism, etc.). In fact, of course, it is not – never has been – a single political and ideological current, let alone a homogeneous social force, possessed of unitary organisation, strategy, programme and goal, but instead a 'movement of movements'. That is, it encompasses a broad, sometimes bewildering spectrum of conviction and agitation, ranging from varieties of economic nationalism promising a better Keynesian yesterday – hence anti-neoliberal rather than anti-capitalist as such – to varieties of socialism projecting a superior, post-capitalist tomorrow. The internationalist ethos of its majority is conveyed by French supporters who, in the spirit of classical socialist tradition, describe themselves as *alter-mondialistes*, signifying that their search is for an alternative, anti-corporate globalisation. This culture of resistance to the New World Order is still less than a decade old and even risked being strangled at birth, as opponents sought to incriminate it as an accessory in the attack on the World Trade Center. But since it has manifestly survived that ideological police operation, now extended to anyone and anything suspected of the taint of 'anti-Americanism' (another of the impostures of the age),[1] it is time to ponder its potential for delivering the systemic alternative to which it aspires.

Writing in the second series of *New Left Review* in 2002, a US militant bemoaned the 'gulf between intellectuals and activists' on the occasions of Seattle and Genoa – the discrepancy, as he saw it, between effervescent mass practice and quiescent, isolated theory.[2] David Graeber spoke in the name of a 'new anarchism' that had, as it were, avenged its widespread displacement by Marxian socialism in the loyalties of the old workers' movement, in the late nineteenth and early twentieth centuries. That a libertarian anarchism is indeed the ideological dominant in the repertoire of alter-globalisation, in the North anyway, is incontestable – and, conjoined with its organisational autonomism, a major part of the problem, not the solution. For in the name of reinventing politics, it winds up evacuating it (the very reason for its original demotion in the ranks of organised labour). Surveying the political scene four years into the new century, Lucio Magri observed:

> The collapse of actually existing socialism, and the eclipse of social democracy as any other kind of socialism, has ... left a void which has been filled by a spontaneism that negates the need for politics in the name of an uncritical faith in the revolt of the 'multitude'. Such a belief is but a mirror vision of faith in progress: neo-anarchism versus neo-liberalism.[3]

Magri's specific reference is obviously to the outstanding theorisation of alter-globalisation thus far: Michael Hardt and Antonio Negri's virtuoso *Empire*. Contra Graeber, it exhibits no lack of intellectual vitality – quite the reverse, a superfluity of it. The enterprise of a utopia for post-capitalist times can only be welcomed; the form it assumes, if not exactly the 'manifesto for global capital' polemicised against by one critic,[4] is ultimately a mutant Browderism: Americanism is, after all, Communism.

Empire boasted the following endorsement:

> What Hardt and Negri offer is nothing less than a rewriting of *The Communist Manifesto* for our

time: *Empire* conclusively demonstrates how global capitalism generates antagonisms that will finally explode its form. This book rings the death-bell not only for the complacent liberal advocates of the 'end of history', but also for pseudo-radical Cultural Studies which avoid the full confrontation with today's capitalism.[5]

No stranger to what Henri Lefebvre once called *l'effort vers l'outrance* – a straining for effect by exaggeration – afflicting many French intellectuals, the author of these lines – Slavoj Žižek, artisan of a quasi-Third Period Marxism–Lacanism – was puffing beyond pastry. *Empire* as 'a rewriting of *The Communist Manifesto* for our time' merits the verdict of a Labour dignitary on his party's 1983 election manifesto: 'the longest suicide note in history'. The empire of capital will not be felled by intimations of multitudinity, flip side of the 'international community' and new 'religion of the subaltern'.[6] A sober prose of the present is infinitely preferable to any such intoxicated poetry of the future, rhapsody in red. Can we look to the minoritarian, more traditionally socialist wing of alter-globalisation for 'a full confrontation with today's capitalism'?

WHAT'S IN A NAME?

The first thing to note is that it at least enjoys the ballast of an emergent, institutionalised rejectionist front, albeit one marginal in the wider scheme of things. In the South, particularly in Latin America, it comprises regimes (Cuba, Venezuela and Bolivia, but not – decisively – Brazil, Argentina or Chile), underscoring (we may note in passing) the pertinence of a sometime dictum of Chairman Mao's: 'It is no use preaching socialism unless you have got a country to practise it in.' In the North – Europe, but definitely not the USA – it encompasses parties (e.g. Rifondazione comunista in Italy or Die Linke in Germany), with a real presence in societies and legislatures alike. As to its ideology, as we saw in Chapter 1, a prominent figure in the 'Globalise Resistance' network, applauding the emergence of an embryonic anti-capitalist movement in 2003, suggested that Marx and Engels's text of 1848 'remains a manifesto for it'.[7] The same year, *An Anti-Capitalist Manifesto* appeared from one of Chris Harman's co-thinkers, the leading British Marxist Alex Callinicos, whose title in a sense speaks for itself.

In his Introduction, Callinicos, disclaiming any 'attempt to improve or update such a classic', acknowledges that his book was 'loosely inspired' by the *Communist Manifesto* – 'the most celebrated statement of Marx's critique of the capitalist mode of production' – and cites its author as a 'major reference point'.[8] Initial puzzlement – if no updating is required, whence the rationale for a new manifesto? – is compounded by closer inspection of the title, which turns out not quite to speak for itself. At the outset, just as Harman had advanced the *Communist Manifesto* as a – not the – manifesto for a contemporary anti-capitalist movement, so Callinicos alerts readers to the fact that 'this is *an* anti-capitalist manifesto: there can and should be many others'. His own arguments, he goes on, 'represent one particular take on what [the anti-capitalist movement] is about – and one that is more influenced by the revolutionary Marxist tradition than probably many would find comfortable'.[9] Given the tradition to which Callinicos advertises adherence, there are two striking things about his title when compared with what became known as *The Communist Manifesto*. The first is that on the one hand we have an indefinite article – '*An* Anti-Capitalist Manifesto' – while on the other we have the definite: '*The* Communist Manifesto'. The second – of greater weight – is that whereas Callinicos's critique of the capitalist mode of production offers a negative formulation – 'An *Anti-Capitalist* Manifesto' – Marx and Engels posted a positive alternative to capitalism on the banner of theirs: 'The *Communist* Manifesto'.

The significance of what might seem like terminological trivia is this. When, decades ago, President Kennedy's adviser W.W. Rostow wrote a work of modernisation theory (*The Stages of Economic Growth*), subtitling it 'A Non-Communist Manifesto', everyone knew that behind the neutral 'non-communist' lay 'anti-communist';[10] that, treating communism as a 'disease of the transition', it was, in intent and effect, a 'Capitalist Manifesto'; but that, back in the 1960s, when a US-led 'Alliance for Progress' was being mounted against anti-imperialist promptings from Havana, the term 'capitalism' was not in good odour, dictating discretion as the better part of valour. Analogously, we may note that behind the negative of Callinicos's title what we are actually dealing with is a socialist manifesto, whose author, in the manner of Marx and Engels's own chapter on 'socialist and communist literature', situates his text with respect to the 'varieties and strategies' of anti-capitalism he inventories, and distinguishes his own position from them. Callinicos demarcates himself from the available alternatives, invoking the 'revolutionary Marxist tradition' of Marx and Engels, Lenin and Trotsky, Luxemburg and Gramsci. However, what he does not do – and this is not a criticism, given the purpose of his book, merely an observation – is to pose the question of how his enterprise relates to the Marxism of the Internationals (the Marxism of the party schools, for militants and masses; not of the intellectuals, for graduate students). In particular, by the criteria of the classical Marxism that defined itself as 'scientific socialism', what is the status of this *Anti-Capitalist Manifesto*? And what, if anything, does that tell us about the anti-capitalism that has its sights set on an alternative globalisation?

Marxian socialism is vulnerable to the criticism that, had the *Communist Manifesto* and the classical Marxist tradition been half-way right, there would be no need for an anti-capitalist manifesto in 2003. A distinct, albeit related, claim will be pressed here:

namely, that there is a profound question mark over the compatibility between initiatives such as Callinicos's, as they wrestle with issues of systemic analysis, strategy, transitional programme and so on, and core contentions of the Marxist tradition. At all events, some of the latter are either wholly absent from, or significantly revised in, his text – and this for the unexceptionable reason that they are unsustainable.

Thus, we encounter no conception of historical materialism as supplying a projection of the trajectory of human history that serves to undergird the socialist project; no sense of Marx's analysis of capitalism as involving its inevitable collapse, let alone its necessary supersession by communism (Callinicos's text only furnishes preconditions for such an outcome); no assignment of a historical mission to the proletariat as the 'universal class'; and no assertion of the bourgeoisie's inability to expand the productive forces, requiring the task to be entrusted to the proletariat. (The stress in alter-globalisation literature is invariably on their destructive overdevelopment – more hypertrophy than atrophy.) Callinicos's inclusions are arguably as telling as his omissions. In the last chapter ('Imagining Other Worlds'), we find him engaged in an endeavour over which Marx, Engels, Lenin, Trotsky and, until very recently, their followers would have cast a decidedly sceptical (even jaundiced) eye – for example, exploring the institutional shape of a 'democratically planned socialist economy' and explicating the values of justice and so forth implicit in contemporary anti-capitalism.

Max Weber once remarked that 'anyone who wants "vision" can go to the cinema'. To win the world to which Callinicos, following Marx, summons readers of his manifesto, 'vision' – not only imagining another world that is possible as well as desirable, but also writing a plausible socialist prescription to complement the diagnosis and prognosis for capitalism – is indispensable. The guarantees of history held out by 'scientific socialism' have been lost; and, contrary to Marx's 1859 Preface, humanity does not only set itself such problems as it can resolve (even where there is a will, there is not necessarily a way). This is not to suggest that everything that was solid about socialism (or that was thought to be solid) has melted into air. The classical diagnosis of the irrationality and inhumanity of capitalism retains full legitimacy. But what, despite its author's intentions, *An Anti-Capitalist Manifesto* betrays is that all actually existing anti-capitalists, for whom an alternative to corporate globalisation worthy of the name would be socialism, are utopians now – even if some are more utopian than others.

ENDS IN SIGHT?

In his Preface to a recent critical history of Marxism, André Tosel has written:

> A for now victorious neo-capitalism has proved
> capable of developing the productive forces at a
> prodigious rate, despite the enormous damage it
> has inflicted on humanity and nature. It has been
> able to legitimate itself as the only possible order by
> reference to the virtues of the market, representative
> democracy, the religion of human rights, and the
> seductions of a generalised consumerism.[11]

Predicated of capitalism in the past tense, these
attributes continue to grace (or disgrace) it in the
present. Meanwhile, however, US foreign policy
has (dys)functioned to open a second front in the
contestation of what Samir Amin calls the civilisation
of 'moneytheism'. Half a decade since the start of
a pre-emptive 'war on terror' carolled by military
humanists ('Oh what a lovely just war!'), it is clear
that imperial expeditions to Kabul and Baghdad have
incited the very furies they were directed at mowing
down with daisy-cutters and assorted technologies.
Moreover, their initial designs have been frustrated
– courtesy not of demonstrations and elections, let
alone Habermas-style op-ed handwringing over a
'divided West', but by a tenacious resistance on the
ground that has to date defied all the odds.

For some (Hobsbawm for example, as we saw in
Chapter 3), what Luciano Canfora has maliciously
dubbed a 'posthumous triumph of the "Brezhnev
doctrine"'[12] is a paradoxical symptom of relative US
decline – a *bellum unium contra omnes* launched by the
Bush administration to shore up the faltering economic

position that belies uncontested military supremacy (no changing of the global guard is in the offing). If so, the identity of the principal competitor is no mystery: offstage for Fukuyama and Hobsbawm, yet to receive the attention promised by Anderson, *la Cina è vicina* (China is close at hand) in a sense altogether unintended and undesired by the Italian Maoists who coined the slogan in the 1960s. The post-1978 'four modernisations', conducted in a spirit of if you can't beat them, join them – and thereby beat them, and producing impetuous capitalist development under nominally communist supervision, have led to a situation in which the artillery of Chinese commodities is today battering down walls, North American included. Accordingly, might it be the case that, in a historical peripeteia flowing from imperial hubris forecast by 1990s 'declinists', the USA is doomed to repeat the trajectory of the UK it supplanted after 1945 – winning the Cold War only to lose the ensuing peace (or what passes for it), and foreshadowing a New World Order in which the New World no longer gives the orders?

Should the mandate of capitalist heaven pass to the People's Republic, in an irony of history that would have defeated Deutscher, it would scarcely enhance the prospects for socialism (outside the dwindling ranks of those who lend credence to Chinese protestations of a 'socialist market economy'). Rather, in the absence of a political liberalisation by Beijing, something approximating to the second scenario envisaged by Fukuyama in 1992 would transpire: the victory of a bureaucratic–authoritarian type of capitalism over the liberal democratic species. Rendering the putatively post-historical world economically homogeneous but politically hybrid, this would not be Fukuyama's preferred terminus.

As for Hobsbawm's and Anderson's preferences, throughout the twentieth century, futures for socialism duly came, and inexorably went, across four continents – so many results without prospects, inscribed in history by their dates: 1917, 1936, 1959, 1968, 1975, 1978 ... At the beginning of the twenty-first century, the cause defended by the premier British socialist intellectuals of their respective generations lies beached by a historical tide now retiring beyond the horizon. While regretting and quarrelling with its effects, neither of them (to switch metaphors) proposes to minimise the scale of a geopolitical earthquake.[13] We have seen Anderson remonstrating with two inadmissible reactions to fin-de-siècle political reality – 'accommodation' and 'consolation' – while allowing for the possibility of a third: 'a lucid recognition of the nature and triumph of the system, without either adaptation or self-deception, but also without any belief in the chance of an alternative to it. A bitter conclusion of this kind is, however, rarely articulated as a public position.'[14] Such a conclusion, however bitter, is not only logically possible, but evidentially defensible and publicly articulable. For of socialist history there is no new beginning, and of capitalist history no final ending, currently in sight.

Notes

PREFACE

1. Maurice Merleau-Ponty, *Signs*, trans. Richard C. McCleary, Evanston, Ill.: Northwestern University Press, 1964, p. 9.
2. Domenico Losurdo, Introduzione to Karl Marx and Friedrich Engels, *Manifesto del partito comunista*, Rome and Bari: Laterza, p. xlvii.

CHAPTER 1

1. John Cassidy, 'The return of Marx', *New Yorker*, 20–27 October 1997; reprinted in *Independent on Sunday*, 7 December 1997.
2. 'In Our Time', BBC Radio 4, broadcast 14 July 2005; *Daily Mail*, 14 July 2005.
3. Eric Hobsbawm, Introduction to Karl Marx and Friedrich Engels, *The Communist Manifesto: A Modern Edition*, London and New York: Verso, 1998, p. 18; Gareth Stedman Jones, Introduction to Karl Marx and Friedrich Engels, *The Communist Manifesto*, London: Penguin, 2002, p. 5.
4. Antonio Labriola, *Essays on the Materialistic Conception of History* (1903), trans. Charles H. Kerr, New York: Monthly Review Press, 1966, pp. 9–10.
5. Labriola, *Essays*, p. 69.
6. Friedrich Engels, *Anti-Dühring: Herr Eugen Dühring's Revolution in Science*, trans. Emile Burns, Moscow: Progress Publishers, 1977, p. 13. Here – the Preface to the Second Edition of 1885 – Engels noted the 'first presentation [of this world-view] in Marx's *Poverty of Philosophy* and in the *Communist Manifesto*'.
7. Karl Marx and Friedrich Engels, *Selected Works*, vol. 3, Moscow: Progress Publishers, Moscow 1977, p. 133.
8. Gian Mario Bravo, 'L'attualità del *Manifesto del partito comunista*', in Bravo (ed.), *Il Manifesto del partito comunista e i suoi interpreti*, Rome: Riuniti, 1973, p. cix.

NOTES

9. See Karl Marx, *Capital: A Critique of Political Economy*, vol. 1, trans. Ben Fowkes, Harmondsworth: Penguin/NLR, 1976, p. 930 n. 2, quoting *Communist Manifesto: Modern Edition*, pp. 50, 47.

10. Marx and Engels, *Communist Manifesto*, p. 193. Marx and Engels nevertheless entertained the possibility of a 'subsequent edition ... bridging the gap from 1847 to the present day' (p. 194). By the time of his Preface to the German Edition of 1883, Engels regretfully noted that in view of Marx's recent death 'there can be even less thought of supplementing or revising the Manifesto' (p. 197).

11. See Engels, 'Preface to the English Edition of 1888', in Marx and Engels, *Communist Manifesto: Modern Edition*, pp. 85–6.

12. Ibid., p. 86.

13. See Karl Marx, 'Preface to *A Contribution to the Critique of Political Economy*', in Karl Marx and Friedrich Engels, *Selected Works*, vol. 1, Moscow: Progress Publishers, 1977, pp. 503–4.

14. Fredric Jameson, *Postmodernism, or The Cultural Logic of Late Capitalism*, London: Verso, 1991, p. 47.

15. Karl Marx, 'Speech at the Anniversary of the *People's Paper*', in Marx and Engels, *Selected Works*, vol. 1, pp. 500–1.

16. 'The bourgeois viewpoint', Marx noted, 'has never advanced beyond this antithesis between itself and this romantic viewpoint, and therefore the latter will accompany it as legitimate antithesis up to its blessed end': Karl Marx, *Grundrisse: Foundations of the Critique of Political Economy*, trans. Martin Nicolaus, Harmondsworth: Penguin/NLR, 1977, p. 162.

17. See Marshall Berman, *All That Is Solid Melts into Air: The Experience of Modernity*, London: Verso, 1983, ch. 2.

18. Marx and Engels, *Communist Manifesto: Modern Edition*, p. 53.

19. Marx and Engels, *Selected Works*, vol. 1, p. 504.

20. Karl Marx, *Early Writings*, trans. Rodney Livingstone and Gregor Benton, Harmondsworth: Penguin/NLR, 1977, p. 348.

21. Marx and Engels, *Communist Manifesto: Modern Edition*, p. 63.

22. Ibid., p. 51.

23. Labriola, *Essays*, p. 14.

24. Marx and Engels, *Communist Manifesto: Modern Edition*, p. 36.

25. Ibid., pp. 37–40.

26. A couple of pages later, Marx precisely makes the equation 'the bourgeoisie, i.e., capital': ibid., p. 42.

27. Ibid., p. 35.

28. Ibid., p. 41.

29. Ibid., p. 42.

30. Ibid., p. 60.

31. Ibid., p. 47.

32. Ibid., p. 42.

33. Ibid., p. 47.

34. Ibid., pp. 49–50.

35. Karl Kautsky, *The Class Struggle (Erfurt Program)* (1892), trans. William E. Bohn, Chicago: Charles H. Kerr, 1910, p. 93.
36. Marx and Engels, *Communist Manifesto: Modern Edition*, p. 35.
37. Ibid., pp. 44–6.
38. Ibid., p. 49.
39. Ibid., pp. 48, 52.
40. Ibid., p. 50.
41. Ibid., p. 35.
42. Marx and Engels, *Selected Works*, vol. 3, p. 151: 'To accomplish this act of universal emancipation is the historical mission of the modern proletariat.'
43. Marx and Engels, *Communist Manifesto: Modern Edition*, p. 60.
44. Ibid., p. 51.
45. Ibid., p. 47.
46. Ibid., p. 49.
47. Ibid., p. 60.
48. Ibid., p. 62.
49. Kautsky, *Class Struggle*, p. 199.
50. Labriola, *Essays*, p. 35.
51. V.I. Lenin, 'The Historical Destiny of the Doctrine of Karl Marx' (1913), trans. Stepan Apreysan, in *Collected Works*, vol. 18, London: Lawrence & Wishart, 1963, p. 582.
52. Rosa Luxemburg, 'Speech at the Founding Convention of the German Communist Party' (1918), trans. Eden and Cedar Paul, in *Rosa Luxemburg Speaks*, ed. Mary-Alice Waters, New York: Pathfinder Press, 1980, pp. 412, 415.
53. Leon Trotsky, 'Ninety Years of the *Communist Manifesto*', in Isaac Deutscher (ed.), *The Age of Permanent Revolution: A Trotsky Anthology*, New York: Dell, 1964, pp. 291, 295.
54. Palmiro Togliatti, 'Saggio sul centenario del Manifesto', in Bravo (ed.), *Manifesto del partito comunista*, p. 471.
55. Labour Party, *Communist Manifesto: Socialist Landmark – A New Appreciation for the Labour Party Written by Harold J. Laski*, London: George Allen and Unwin, 1948, p. 101.
56. Eduard Bernstein, *The Preconditions of Socialism* (1899), ed. and trans. Henry Tudor, Cambridge: Cambridge University Press, 1993, p. 201.
57. Karl Marx and Friedrich Engels, *Collected Works*, vol. 5, London: Lawrence & Wishart, 1976, p. 49; emphasis in the original.
58. Marx and Engels, *Selected Works*, vol. 1, p. 501.
59. E.J. Hobsbawm, 'Intellectuals and the Class Struggle', in *Revolutionaries: Contemporary Essays*, London: Phoenix, 1994, pp. 256–7.
60. See Domenico Losurdo, Introduzione to Karl Marx and Friedrich Engels, *Manifesto del partito comunista*, Rome and Bari: Laterza, 1999, p. xlvi.
61. See Hobsbawm, Introduction, pp. 22–3, 25.
62. Kautsky, *Class Struggle*, p. 118.

63. 'We now realize the absolute truth of the statement formulated for the first time by Marx and Engels as the scientific basis of socialism in the great charter of our movement, the *Communist Manifesto*. Socialism, they said, will become a historical necessity. Socialism is inevitable not merely because proletarians are no longer willing to live under the conditions imposed by the capitalist class, but further because, if the proletariat fails to fulfil its duties as a class, if it fails to realize socialism, we shall crash down to a common doom': *Rosa Luxemburg Speaks*, p. 412.
64. Lenin, *Collected Works*, vol. 18, p. 582.
65. See Marx, *Early Writings*, pp. 256–7.
66. Karl Marx and Friedrich Engels, *Collected Works*, vol. 4, London: Lawrence & Wishart, 1975, p. 37.
67. Karl Marx and Friedrich Engels, *Selected Correspondence*, trans. I. Lasker, Moscow: Progress Publishers, 1975, p. 294.
68. *Communist Manifesto: Modern Edition*, p. 58.
69. See Losurdo, Introduzione, p. xxxiv.
70. Marx, *Capital*, vol. 1, pp. 90, 921. Cf. Antonio Gramsci, 'The Revolution against "Capital"' (1917), in *Selections from the Political Writings (1910–1920)*, ed. Quintin Hoare and trans. John Mathews, London: Lawrence & Wishart, 1977, pp. 34–7.
71. Marx and Engels, 'Preface to the Russian Edition of 1882', in *Communist Manifesto*, p. 196.
72. See Costanzo Preve, *Storia critica del marxismo. Dalla nascita di Karl Marx alla dissoluzione del comunismo storico novecentesco (1818–1991)*, Naples: La Città del Sole, 2007, p. 234.
73. Marx, *Capital*, vol. 1, p. 99.
74. See, in addition to his *Storia critica del marxismo*, Costanzo Preve, *Marx inattuale. Eredità e prospettiva*, Turin: Bollati Boringhieri, 2004.
75. Antonio Gramsci, *Selections from the Prison Notebooks*, ed. and trans. Quintin Hoare and Geoffrey Nowell Smith, London: Lawrence & Wishart, 1971, p. 337.
76. Cf. Chris Harman, Introduction to Karl Marx and Friedrich Engels, *The Communist Manifesto*, London: Bookmarks, 2003, p. 4.
77. Geoff Eley, *Forging Democracy: The History of the Left in Europe, 1850–2000*, Oxford: Oxford University Press, 2002, p. 37.

CHAPTER 2

1. Francis Fukuyama, *The End of History and the Last Man*, 2nd US edn, New York: Free Press, 2006, p. 341.
2. Fukuyama, *End of History*, p. 346.
3. Francis Fukuyama, 'No short cut on the road to democracy', *Scotsman*, 3 April 2007.

4. See Francis Fukuyama, *After the Neocons: America at the Crossroads*, London: Profile Books, 2006. Cf. Perry Anderson's review, 'Inside man', *Nation*, 24 April 2006.

5. Francis Fukuyama, 'The End of History?', *The National Interest*, no. 16, Summer 1989, p. 3.

6. Ibid., pp. 3–4.

7. Ibid., pp. 16, 8.

8. G.W.F. Hegel, *The Philosophy of History*, trans. J. Sibree, New York: Dover, 1956, p. 19.

9. Fukuyama, 'End of History?', p. 3.

10. Ibid., p. 9.

11. G.V. Plekhanov, *Socialism and the Political Struggle*, quoted in Adam Westoby, *The Evolution of Communism*, Cambridge: Polity Press, 1989, p. ii.

12. Fukuyama, 'End of History?', p. 9.

13. Ibid., p. 18.

14. Ibid., p. 4.

15. Alexandre Kojève, *Introduction to the Reading of Hegel: Lectures on 'The Phenomenology of Spirit'*, ed. Allan Bloom and trans. James H. Nichols Jr., Ithaca, N.Y.: Cornell University Press, 1980, p. 185. The maxim is cited in Fukuyama, *End of History*, p. 137.

16. See Kojève, 'Note to the Second Edition', in *Hegel*, pp. 159–62. And cf. Fukuyama, 'End of History?', p. 5, n. 3.

17. See, for example, Hobsbawm's offhand dismissal in 'Goodbye to All That', in Robin Blackburn (ed.), *After the Fall: The Failure of Communism and the Future of Socialism*, London and New York: Verso, 1991, p. 124. We shall return to this in Chapter 3.

18. See Perry Anderson, 'The Ends of History', in *A Zone of Engagement*, London and New York: Verso, 1992, p. 345: 'The charge heard on the Right, of an inverted Marxism, is grounds for tribute on the Left.'

19. Fukuyama, *End of History*, p. xiii.

20. Ibid., pp. xii–xiii.

21. Ibid., p. xiv.

22. Ibid., p. xv.

23. Ibid., p. xvi.

24. Ibid., p. 144.

25. Ibid., pp. xvi–xvii.

26. Ibid., p. xviii.

27. Ibid., p. xix.

28. Ibid., pp. xxii–xxiii.

29. Ibid., p. 45.

30. See ibid., pp. 45–6. In a note anticipating the stance of *After the Neocons*, Fukuyama observes: 'They can, of course, challenge liberal democracy through terrorist bombs and bullets, a significant but not vital challenge' (p. 361 n. 9).

31. Ibid., p. 48.

32. Ibid., p. 90.

33. Ibid., p. 112.
34. Ibid., p. 129.
35. Ibid., p. 123.
36. Ibid., p. 131.
37. Ibid., p. 135.
38. Ibid., p. 204; emphasis added.
39. Ibid., p. 125.
40. Ibid., p. 229.
41. Ibid., pp. 233, 242.
42. Ibid., p. 238.
43. Cited in ibid., p. 66.
44. Ibid., p. 278.
45. Ibid., p. 280.
46. Ibid., pp. 279–80.
47. Ibid., p. 289.
48. Ibid., p. 292.
49. Ibid., p. 293.
50. Ibid., p. 314.
51. Ibid., p. 334; emphasis in original.
52. Ibid., p. 338.
53. See Joseph McCarney, 'Endgame', *Radical Philosophy*, no. 62, Autumn 1992; and cf. McCarney, 'Shaping Ends: Reflections on Fukuyama', *New Left Review*, no. 202, November/December 1993.
54. See Alex Callinicos, *Theories and Narratives: Reflections on the Philosophy of History*, Cambridge: Polity Press, 1994, ch. 1: here p. 38.
55. See Karl Marx, *Capital: A Critique of Political Economy*, vol. 1, trans. Ben Fowkes, Harmondsworth: Penguin/NLR, 1976, pp. 102–3.
56. Fukuyama, *End of History*, p. 130.
57. Ibid., p. 56.
58. Ibid., p. 139.
59. Ibid., p. xv. The image is repeated on p. 134.
60. Louis Althusser and Étienne Balibar, *Reading 'Capital'*, trans. Ben Brewster, London: New Left Books, 1970, p. 120.
61. See Louis Althusser, *The Spectre of Hegel: Early Writings*, ed. François Matheron and trans. G.M. Goshgarian, London and New York: Verso, 1997, pp. 206–9.
62. Cf. Fukuyama, *End of History*, p. xviii.
63. Anderson, *Zone of Engagement*, p. 336.
64. See Callinicos, *Theories and Narratives*, especially pp. 17–21, criticising Deutscherite reactions to Fukuyama by Anderson, Fred Halliday and the present author.
65. Cf., however, Alex Callinicos, *The Revenge of History: Marxism and the East European Revolutions*, Cambridge: Polity Press, 1991, for an argument to the contrary.
66. Jorge Semprun is quoted from *Le Monde*, 15 October 1991, in Emmanuel Terray, *Le troisième jour du communisme*, Arles: Actes Sud, 1992, p.

92. Terray notes the echo of Sartre's Preface to *Critique of Dialectical Reason*, vol. 1, trans. Alan Sheridan-Smith and ed. Jonathan Rée, London: New Left Books, 1976, p. 822.

67. Kojève, *Hegel*, p. 185. Cf. Vincent Descombes, *Modern French Philosophy*, trans. L. Scott-Fox and J.M. Harding, Cambridge: Cambridge University Press, 1980, p. 14.

68. Fukuyama, *End of History*, p. 336.

69. Ibid., p. xvii. Cf. pp. 25, 48, 153, 200.

70. In his 2006 Afterword, Fukuyama himself notes that '[t]he US ... was born with the birth defect of slavery, which was approved by democratic majorities and enshrined in its constitution': ibid., p. 350.

71. Ibid., p. 245.

72. Ibid., p. 250.

73. W.C. Sellar and R.J. Yeatman, *1066 and All That*, London: Macmillan, 1930, p. 113. The relevant chapter is entitled 'A Bad Thing'.

CHAPTER 3

1. Eric Hobsbawm, *Globalisation, Democracy and Terrorism*, London: Little, Brown, 2007, p. 1.

2. See Eric Hobsbawm, 'Goodbye to All That', in Robin Blackburn (ed.), *After the Fall: The Failure of Communism and the Future of Socialism*, London and New York: Verso, 1991, p. 124; *The New Century*, trans. Allan Cameron, London: Little, Brown, 2000, pp. 114, 166.

3. See Perry Anderson, 'Darkness falls', *Guardian*, 8 November 1994 ('his masterpiece') and Göran Therborn, 'The Autobiography of the Twentieth Century', *New Left Review*, no. 214, November/December 1995, p. 90 ('the masterpiece of an epochal oeuvre'). Anderson's assessment is reiterated in the lengthy essays devoted to Hobsbawm in the *London Review of Books* and reprinted as 'The Vanquished Left: Eric Hobsbawm', in *Spectrum: From Right to Left in the World of Ideas*, London and New York: Verso, 2005, ch. 13: 'There is no doubt at all that *Age of Extremes* is Hobsbawm's masterpiece' (pp. 298–9).

4. Tony Judt, 'Downhill all the way', *New York Review of Books*, 25 May 1995.

5. Eric Hobsbawm, *Age of Extremes: The Short Twentieth Century 1914–1991*, London: Michael Joseph, 1994, pp. ix–x.

6. Eric Hobsbawm, *Revolutionaries: Contemporary Essays*, London: Phoenix, 1994, p. vii.

7. Hobsbawm, *Revolutionaries*, pp. 250–1. Attesting to the consistency of Hobsbawm's sentiments on this score is a passage written 25 years later: 'the sense of a civilization in the convulsions of profound crisis, a world beyond restoration or reform by old procedures which were visibly failing, formed part of the social experience of intellectuals in many parts of Europe. To choose between ruin and revolution – from Right or Left – between no future and a future, seemed, not an abstract

NOTES

choice, but a recognition of how serious the situation was' ('History and Illusion', *New Left Review*, no. 220, November/December 1996, p. 121).

8. Eric Hobsbawm, *Echoes of the Marseillaise: Two Centuries Look Back on the French Revolution*, London and New York: Verso, 1990, p. xiv.

9. Raymond Aron, *The Opium of the Intellectuals*, trans. Terence Kilmartin, London: Secker and Warburg, 1957, pp. xviii, 283.

10. Eric Hobsbawm, *Interesting Times: A Twentieth-Century Life*, London: Allen Lane, 2002, p. 218.

11. Hobsbawm, 'History and Illusion', p. 125.

12. Hobsbawm, *Interesting Times*, p. xiii.

13. Eric Hobsbawm, *The Age of Empire 1875–1914*, London: Weidenfeld & Nicolson, 1995, pp. 8–10.

14. Eric Hobsbawm, *The Age of Revolution 1789–1848*, London: Weidenfeld & Nicolson, 1995, pp. 234–5.

15. Hobsbawm, *Age of Revolution*, pp. 244–5.

16. See Hobsbawm, *Age of Empire*, p. 340. Earlier in his epilogue (p. 330), Hobsbawm writes: 'In terms of the material improvement of the lot of humanity, not to mention of human understanding and control over nature, the case for seeing the history of the twentieth century as progress is actually rather more compelling than it was in the nineteenth. ... But the reasons why we have got out of the habit of thinking of our history as progress are obvious. For when twentieth-century progress is most undeniable, prediction suggests not a continued ascent, but the possibility, perhaps even the imminence, of some catastrophe. ... We have been taught by the experience of our century to live in the expectation of apocalypse.'

17. Hobsbawm, *Age of Extremes*, pp. 584–5. The metaphor had already been employed prior to the fall of the Berlin Wall, in the Preface to Hobsbawm's *Politics for a Rational Left: Political Writing 1977–1988*, London and New York: Verso, 1989, p. 5, where the alternative to contemporary capitalism had been identified as 'the necessary supersession of this system – or ... a relapse into the ages of darkness'.

18. Eric Hobsbawm, 'Barbarism: A User's Guide', reprinted in *On History*, London: Abacus, 1988, p. 335.

19. Hobsbawm, *Age of Extremes*, p. 6.

20. Ibid., p. 497. On the penultimate page of the book, Hobsbawm likewise retracts the guarded optimism evinced in the conclusion to *The Age of Empire*: 'There is less reason to feel hopeful about the future than in the middle 1980s.'

21. Anderson, 'Darkness falls'.

22. Hobsbawm, *Age of Extremes*, pp. 10, 11.

23. See Simon Bromley, 'The Long Twentieth Century', *Radical Philosophy*, no. 77, May/June 1996.

24. Hobsbawm, *Age of Extremes*, p. 270.

25. Ibid., p. 498.

26. Hobsbawm, *Interesting Times*, pp. 127, 56.
27. Hobsbawm, *Age of Extremes*, p. 84.
28. Ibid., p. 7.
29. Francis Mulhern; personal communication.
30. Hobsbawm, *Age of Extremes*, p. 144. For Hobsbawm's balance sheet of Popular Frontism, see 'Fifty Years of Popular Fronts', in *Politics for a Rational Left*, ch. 9; and cf. his 'Gli intellettuali e l'anti-fascismo', in Eric Hobsbawm et al. (eds), *Storia del marxismo*, vol. 3, part 2, Turin: Einaudi, 1981 (a text seemingly unpublished in English).
31. Hobsbawm, *Age of Extremes*, p. 498.
32. Ibid., p. 563.
33. Ibid., p. 17.
34. Ibid., pp. 558–9.
35. Cf. Joseph Schumpeter, *Capitalism, Socialism and Democracy*, London: Routledge, 1994, p. 139: 'In breaking down the pre-capitalist framework of society, capitalism thus broke not only barriers that impeded its progress, but also flying buttresses that prevented its collapse.' See also p. 162.
36. Hobsbawm, *Interesting Times*, p. 83.
37. See also Justin Rosenberg, 'Hobsbawm's Century', *Monthly Review*, vol. 47, no. 3, 1995.
38. Eric Hobsbawm, *Industry and Empire: From 1750 to the Present Day*, Harmondsworth: Penguin, 1983, p. 225: 'The characteristic attitude of British or other governments towards the economy before the Industrial Revolution was that they had a duty to do something about it. This is the almost universal attitude of governments towards the economy today. But between these two eras, which represent what might be called the norm of history, and indeed of reason, there occurred an age in which the fundamental attitude of the government and the economists was the opposite: the less it could manage to intervene in the economy, the better. ... The history of government economic policy and theory since the Industrial Revolution is essentially that of the rise and fall of *laissez-faire*.'
39. Hobsbawm, *Interesting Times*, p. 137.
40. Hobsbawm, *Age of Extremes*, p. 559.
41. Hobsbawm, *The New Century*, p. 49.
42. Hobsbawm, *Interesting Times*, p. 412. Alluding to Western support for Afghani jihadists in the 1980s, Hobsbawm legitimately reflects that '[t]he world may yet regret that, faced with Rosa Luxemburg's alternative of socialism or barbarism, it decided against socialism' (p. 281).
43. See Hobsbawm, *Globalisation, Democracy and Terrorism*, pp. 7ff.
44. Ibid., p. 46.
45. Ibid., pp. 70–1.
46. Ibid., p. 137.
47. Ibid., p. 161; see also p. 47.
48. See ibid., p. 164.

49. See ibid., pp. 47, 162.
50. As Ellen Meiksins Wood remarked in 2003, '[w]hat we are seeing today, as the Bush administration pursues its reckless policies, may be a special kind of madness; but, if so, it is a madness firmly rooted not only in the past half-century of US history, but in the systemic logic of capitalism': *Empire of Capital*, London and New York: Verso, 2003, p. x.
51. Eric Hobsbawm, Introduction to Karl Marx and Friedrich Engels, *The Communist Manifesto: A Modern Edition*, London and New York: Verso, 1998, pp. 28–9.
52. See Marx and Engels, *Communist Manifesto: A Modern Edition*, p. 35.
53. See Anderson, *Spectrum*, p. 316.

CHAPTER 4

1. See Perry Anderson, *Considerations on Western Marxism*, London: New Left Books, 1976, pp. 95–106; and cf. Perry Anderson, 'Trotsky's Interpretation of Stalinism', in Tariq Ali (ed.), *The Stalinist Legacy: Its Impact on Twentieth-Century World Politics*, Harmondsworth: Penguin, 1984. For my own attempt at an overview, see *Perry Anderson: The Merciless Laboratory of History*, Minneapolis: University of Minnesota Press, 1998.
2. 'The Russian Revolution [was] ... the inaugural incarnation of a new kind of history, founded on an unprecedented form of agency. Notoriously, the results of the great cycle of upheavals it initiated have to date been far from those expected at their outset. But the alteration of the potential of historical action, in the course of the 20th century, remains irreversible': Perry Anderson, *Arguments Within English Marxism*, London: New Left Books, 1980, pp. 20–1.
3. Perry Anderson, *In the Tracks of Historical Materialism*, London: New Left Books, 1983, pp. 68–9.
4. Perry Anderson, letter of 12 December 1988, in Perry Anderson and Norberto Bobbio, 'Un carteggio tra Norberto Bobbio e Perry Anderson', *Teoria Politica*, vol. 5, nos 2–3, 1989, pp. 293–308.
5. See Perry Anderson, 'The Ends of History', in *A Zone of Engagement*, London and New York: Verso, 1992, ch. 13.
6. See Perry Anderson, 'Marshall Berman: Modernity and Revolution', in *A Zone of Engagement*, ch. 2; esp. pp. 45, 48–9.
7. Perry Anderson, *The Origins of Postmodernity*, London and New York: Verso, 1998, p. 66.
8. Ibid., p. 118.
9. Ibid., pp. 91–2.
10. Perry Anderson, 'Renewals', *New Left Review*, 2nd series, no. 1, January/February 2000, p. 7.
11. Ibid., p. 8.

12. Ibid., p. 10.

13. Ibid., p. 11.

14. Ibid., pp. 13–14. And cf. Perry Anderson, 'The Vanquished Left: Eric Hobsbawm', in *Spectrum: From Right to Left in the World of Ideas*, London and New York: Verso, 2005, ch. 13; esp. p. 316.

15. Anderson, 'Renewals', p. 13, n. 5.

16. Ibid., p. 14.

17. Ibid., p. 16.

18. Ibid., p. 17.

19. Ibid., p. 20.

20. Ibid., p. 19.

21. Ibid., p. 17. Indicative of that discontinuity in Anderson's own case is the fact that no further instalment of the history project initiated more than 30 years ago, with *Passages from Antiquity to Feudalism* and *Lineages of the Absolutist State*, has appeared; while three signature titles – *Considerations on Western Marxism*, *Arguments Within English Marxism*, and *In the Tracks of Historical Materialism* – have long been out of print.

22. Ibid., pp. 16–17.

23. Ibid., p. 19.

24. Jean-François Lyotard, 'Note on the Meaning of "Post-"', in *The Postmodern Explained to Children*, London: Turnaround, 1998, p. 91.

25. See Boris Kagarlitsky, 'The Suicide of *New Left Review*', *International Socialism*, no. 88, Autumn 2000.

26. Anderson, 'Renewals', p. 14.

27. Quoted in Matthew Price, 'The new new thing', *Lingua Franca*, February 2001, p. 21.

28. Gilbert Achcar, 'The "Historical Pessimism" of Perry Anderson', *International Socialism*, no. 88, Autumn 2000, p. 140.

29. Ibid., p. 136. For analogous verdicts, see the subsequent books by Paul Blackledge, *Perry Anderson, Marxism and the New Left*, London: Merlin Press, 2004, ch. 7; and Duncan Thompson, *Pessimism of the Intellect? A History of New Left Review*, London: Merlin Press, 2007, pp. 157–8.

30. Anderson, *Postmodernity*, pp. 76–7.

31. Fredric Jameson, *Marxism and Form: Twentieth-Century Dialectical Theories of Literature*, Princeton: Princeton University Press, 1974, p. 273; cited in Anderson, *Postmodernity*, p. 90.

32. Perry Anderson, 'Force and Consent', *New Left Review*, 2nd series, no. 17, September/October 2002, p. 30.

33. Perry Anderson, 'Casuistries of peace and war', *London Review of Books*, 6 March 2003, pp. 12–13.

34. Perry Anderson, 'La batalla de ideas en la construcción de alternativas', August 2003 (available on the web-site of América Latin en Movimiento at http://alainet.org).

35. Anderson, *Postmodernity*, pp. 136–7.

36. Perry Anderson, *English Questions*, London and New York: Verso, 1992, p. 12.
37. Anderson, *Spectrum*, p. 319.

CONCLUSION

1. See Domenico Losurdo, *Il linguaggio dell'Impero. Lessico dell'ideologia americana*, Rome and Bari: Laterza, 2007, ch. 3.
2. David Graeber, 'The New Anarchists', *New Left Review*, 2nd series, no. 13, January/February 2002, p. 61.
3. Lucio Magri, 'Parting Words', trans. Alan O'Leary, *New Left Review*, 2nd series, no. 31, January/February 2005, p. 103.
4. See Ellen Meiksins Wood, 'A Manifesto for Global Capital?', in Gopal Balakrishnan (ed.), *Debating Empire*, London and New York: Verso, 2003.
5. See Michael Hardt and Antonio Negri, *Empire*, Cambridge, Mass. and London: Harvard University Press, 2000; back cover.
6. Antonio Gramsci, *Selections from the Prison Notebooks*, ed. and trans. Quintin Hoare and Geoffrey Nowell Smith, London: Lawrence & Wishart, 1971, p. 337.
7. Chris Harman, Introduction to Karl Marx and Friedrich Engels, *The Communist Manifesto*, London: Bookmarks, p. 4.
8. Alex Callinicos, *An Anti-Capitalist Manifesto*, Cambridge: Polity Press, 2003, p. 20.
9. Ibid., p. 20.
10. Thus, in a rare lapse, Hobsbawm writes of Rostow's book as 'a self-described "anti-Communist Manifesto"': *Interesting Times: A Twentieth-Century Life*, London: Allen Lane, 2002, p. 390.
11. André Tosel, Prefazione to Costanzo Preve, *Storia critica del marxismo. Dalla nascita di Karl Marx all dissoluzione del comunismo storico novecentesco (1818–1991)*, Naples: La Città del Sole, 2007, p. 18.
12. Luciano Canfora, *Esportare la libertà. Il mito che ha fallito*, Milan: Mondadori, 2007, p. 74.
13. Cf. Hobsbawm's 1989 Preface to *Echoes of the Marseillaise: Two Centuries Look Back on the French Revolution*, London and New York: Verso, 1990, p. xv: 'as the great Danish literary critic, Georg Brandes, said à propos of Hippolyte Taine's impassioned attack on the [French] Revolution in his *Origins of Contemporary France*, what is the point of preaching a sermon against an earthquake? (Or in favour of it?)'
14. Perry Anderson, 'Renewals', *New Left Review*, 2nd series, no. 1, January/February 2000, p. 13, n. 5.

Bibliography

Achcar, Gilbert, 'The "Historical Pessimism" of Perry Anderson', *International Socialism*, no. 88, Autumn 2000.

Althusser, Louis, *The Spectre of Hegel: Early Writings*, ed. François Matheron and trans. G.M. Goshgarian (London and New York: Verso, 1997).

—— and Balibar, Étienne, *Reading 'Capital'*, trans. Ben Brewster (London: New Left Books, 1970).

Anderson, Perry, *Arguments Within English Marxism* (London: New Left Books, 1980).

—— 'La batalla de ideas en la construcción de alternativas' (web-site of América Latin en Movimento at http://alainet.org).

—— 'Casuistries of peace and war', *London Review of Books*, 6 March 2003.

—— *Considerations on Western Marxism* (London: New Left Books, 1976).

—— 'Darkness falls', *Guardian*, 8 November 1994.

—— *English Questions* (London and New York: Verso, 1992).

—— 'Force and Consent', *New Left Review*, 2nd series, no. 17, September/October 2002

—— 'Inside man', *Nation*, 24 April 2006.

—— *In the Tracks of Historical Materialism* (London: New Left Books, 1983).

—— *The Origins of Postmodernity* (London and New York: Verso, 1998).

—— 'Renewals', *New Left Review*, 2nd series, no. 1, January/February 2000.

—— *Spectrum: From Right to Left in the World of Ideas* (London and New York: Verso, 2005).

—— 'Trotsky's Interpretation of Stalinism', in Tariq Ali (ed.), *The Stalinist Legacy: Its Impact on Twentieth-Century World Politics* (Harmondsworth: Penguin, 1984).

—— *A Zone of Engagement* (London and New York: Verso, 1992).

—— and Bobbio, Norberto, 'Un carteggio tra Norberto Bobbio e Perry Anderson', *Teoria Politica*, vol. 5, nos 2–3, 1989.

BIBLIOGRAPHY

Aron, Raymond, *The Opium of the Intellectuals*, trans. Terence Kilmartin (London: Secker & Warburg, 1957).

Berman, Marshall, *All That Is Solid Melts into Air: The Experience of Modernity* (London: Verso, 1983).

Bernstein, Eduard, *The Preconditions of Socialism*, ed. and trans. Henry Tudor (Cambridge: Cambridge University Press, 1993).

Blackledge, Paul, *Perry Anderson, Marxism and the New Left* (London: Merlin Press, 2004).

Bravo, Gian Mario (ed.), *Il Manifesto del partito comunista e i suoi interpreti* (Rome: Riuniti, 1973).

Bromley, Simon, 'The Long Twentieth Century', *Radical Philosophy*, no. 77, May/June 1996.

Callinicos, Alex, *An Anti-Capitalist Manifesto* (Cambridge: Polity Press, 2003).

—— *The Revenge of History: Marxism and the East European Revolutions* (Cambridge: Polity Press, 1991).

—— *Theories and Narratives: Reflections on the Philosophy of History* (Cambridge: Polity Press, 1994).

Canfora, Luciano, *Esportare la libertà. Il mito che ha fallito* (Milan: Mondadori, 2007).

Cassidy, John, 'The return of Marx', *New Yorker*, 20–27 October 1997 (reprinted in *Independent on Sunday*, 7 December 1997).

Descombes, Vincent, *Modern French Philosophy*, trans. L. Scott-Fox and J.M. Harding (Cambridge: Cambridge University Press, 1980).

Eley, Geoff, *Forging Democracy: The History of the Left in Europe, 1850–2000* (Oxford: Oxford University Press, 2002).

Elliott, Gregory, *Perry Anderson: The Merciless Laboratory of History* (Minneapolis: University of Minnesota Press, 1998).

Engels, Friedrich, *Anti-Dühring: Herr Eugen Dühring's Revolution in Science*, trans. Emile Burns (Moscow: Progress Publishers, 1977).

Fukuyama, Francis, *After the Neocons: America at the Crossroads* (London: Profile Books, 2006).

—— 'The End of History?', *The National Interest*, no. 16, Summer 1989.

—— *The End of History and the Last Man* (2nd US edn, New York: Free Press, 2006).

—— 'No short cut on the road to democracy', *Scotsman*, 3 April 2007.

Graeber, David, 'The New Anarchists', *New Left Review*, 2nd series, no. 13, January/February 2002.

Gramsci, Antonio, 'The Revolution against "Capital"', in *Selections from the Political Writings (1910–1920)*, ed. Quintin Hoare and trans. John Mathews (London: Lawrence & Wishart, 1977).

—— *Selections from the Prison Notebooks*, ed. and trans. Quintin Hoare and Geoffrey Nowell Smith (London: Lawrence & Wishart, 1971).

Hardt, Michael, and Negri, Antonio, *Empire* (Cambridge, Mass. and London: Harvard University Press, 2000).

Harman, Chris, Introduction to Karl Marx and Friedrich Engels, *The Communist Manifesto* (London: Bookmarks, 2003).

Hegel, G.W.F., *The Philosophy of History*, trans. J. Sibree (New York: Dover, 1956).

Hobsbawm, Eric, *The Age of Capital 1848–1875* (London: Weidenfeld & Nicolson, 1995).

—— *The Age of Empire 1875–1914* (London: Weidenfeld & Nicolson, 1995).

—— *Age of Extremes: The Short Twentieth Century 1914–1991* (London: Michael Joseph, 1994).

—— *The Age of Revolution 1789–1848* (London: Weidenfeld & Nicolson, 1995).

—— *Echoes of the Marseillaise: Two Centuries Look Back on the French Revolution* (London and New York: Verso, 1990).

—— 'Gli intellettuali e l'antifascismo', in Hobsbawm et al. (eds), *Storia del marxismo*, vol. 3, part 2 (Turin: Einaudi, 1981).

—— *Globalisation, Democracy and Terrorism* (London: Little, Brown, 2007).

—— 'Goodbye to All That', in Robin Blackburn (ed.), *After the Fall: The Failure of Communism and the Future of Socialism* (London and New York: Verso, 1991).

—— 'History and Illusion', *New Left Review*, no. 220, November/December 1996.

—— *Industry and Empire: From 1750 to the Present Day* (Harmondsworth: Penguin, 1983).

—— *Interesting Times: A Twentieth-Century Life* (London: Allen Lane, 2002).

—— Introduction to Karl Marx and Friedrich Engels, *The Communist Manifesto: A Modern Edition* (London and New York: Verso, 1998).

—— *The New Century*, trans. Allan Cameron (London: Little, Brown, 2000).

—— *On History* (London: Abacus, 1998).

—— *Politics for a Rational Left: Political Writing 1977–1988* (London and New York: Verso, 1989).

—— *Revolutionaries: Contemporary Essays* (London: Phoenix, 1994).

'In Our Time', BBC Radio 4, broadcast 14 July 2005.

Jameson, Fredric, *Marxism and Form: Twentieth-Century Dialectical Theories of Literature* (Princeton: Princeton University Press, 1974).

—— *Postmodernism, or the Cultural Logic of Late Capitalism* (London: Verso, 1991).

Judt, Tony, 'Downhill all the way', *New York Review of Books*, 25 May 1995.

Kagarlitsky, Boris, 'The Suicide of *New Left Review*', *International Socialism*, no. 88, Autumn 2000.

Kautsky, Karl, *The Class Struggle (Erfurt Program)*, trans. William E. Bohn (Chicago: Charles H. Kerr, 1910).

BIBLIOGRAPHY

Kojève, Alexandre, *Introduction to the Reading of Hegel: Lectures on 'The Phenomenology of Spirit'*, ed. Allan Bloom and trans. James H. Nichols Jr. (Ithaca, N.Y.: Cornell University Press, 1980).

Labour Party, *Communist Manifesto: Socialist Landmark – A New Appreciation Written for the Labour Party by Harold J. Laski* (London: George Allen and Unwin, 1948).

Labriola, Antonio, *Essays on the Materialistic Conception of History*, trans. Charles H. Kerr (New York: Monthly Review Press, 1966).

Lenin, V.I., 'The Historical Destiny of the Doctrine of Karl Marx', trans. Stepan Apreysan, *Collected Works*, vol. 18 (London: Lawrence & Wishart, 1963).

Losurdo, Domenico, Introduzione to Karl Marx and Friedrich Engels, *Manifesto del partito comunista* (Rome and Bari: Laterza, 1999).

—— *Il linguaggio dell'Impero. Lessico dell'ideologia americana* (Rome and Bari: Laterza, 2007).

Luxemburg, Rosa, *Rosa Luxemburg Speaks*, ed. Mary-Alice Waters (New York: Pathfinder Press, 1980).

Lyotard, Jean-François, 'Note on the Meaning of "Post-"', in *The Postmodern Explained to Children* (London: Turnaround, 1998).

Magri, Lucio, 'Parting Words', trans. Alan O'Leary, *New Left Review*, 2nd series, no. 31, January/February 2005.

Marx, Karl, *Capital: A Critique of Political Economy*, vol. 1, trans. Ben Fowkes (Harmondsworth: Penguin/NLR, 1976).

—— *Early Writings*, trans. Rodney Livingstone and Gregor Benton (Harmondsworth: Penguin/NLR, 1977).

—— *Grundrisse: Foundations of the Critique of Political Economy*, trans. Martin Nicolaus (Harmondsworth: Penguin/NLR, 1977).

—— and Engels, Friedrich, *Collected Works*, vol. 4 (London: Lawrence & Wishart, 1975).

—— —— *Collected Works*, vol. 5 (London: Lawrence & Wishart, 1976).

—— —— *The Communist Manifesto* (London: Penguin, 2002).

—— —— *The Communist Manifesto: A Modern Edition* (London and New York: Verso, 1998).

—— —— *Selected Correspondence*, trans. I. Lasker (Moscow: Progress Publishers, 1975).

—— —— *Selected Works*, vol. 1 (Moscow: Progress Publishers, 1977).

—— —— *Selected Works*, vol. 3 (Moscow: Progress Publishers, 1977).

McCarney, Joseph, 'Endgame', *Radical Philosophy*, no. 62, Autumn 1992.

—— 'Shaping Ends: Reflections on Fukuyama', *New Left Review*, no. 202, November/December 1993.

Merleau-Ponty, Maurice, *Signs*, trans. Richard C. McCleary (Evanston, Ill.: Northwestern University Press, 1964).

Preve, Costanzo, *Marx inattuale. Eredità e prospettiva* (Turin: Bollati Boringhieri, 2004).

—— *Storia critica del marxismo. Dalla nascita di Karl Marx all dissoluzione del comunismo storico novecentesco (1818–1991)* (Naples: La Città del Sole, 2007).

Price, Matthew, 'The new new thing', *Lingua Franca*, February 2001.

Rosenberg, Justin, 'Hobsbawm's Century', *Monthly Review*, vol. 47, no. 3, 1995.

Sartre, Jean-Paul, *Critique of Dialectical Reason*, vol. 1, trans. Alan Sheridan-Smith and ed. Jonathan Rée (London: New Left Books, 1976).

Schumpeter, Joseph A., *Capitalism, Socialism and Democracy* (London: Routledge, 1994).

Sellar, W.C. and Yeatman, R.J., *1066 and All That* (London: Macmillan, 1930).

Stedman Jones, Gareth, Introduction to Karl Marx and Friedrich Engels, *The Communist Manifesto* (London: Penguin, 2002).

Terray, Emmanuel, *Le troisième jour du communisme* (Arles: Actes Sud, 1992).

Therborn, Göran, 'The Autobiography of the Twentieth Century', *New Left Review*, no. 214, November/December 1995.

Thompson, Duncan, *Pessimism of the Intellect? A History of New Left Review* (London: Merlin Press, 2007).

Togliatti, Palmiro, 'Saggio sul centenario del Manifesto', in Gian Mario Bravo (ed.), *Il Manifesto del partito comunista e i suoi interpreti* (Rome: Riuniti, 1973).

Trotsky, Leon, 'Ninety Years of the *Communist Manifesto*', in Isaac Deutscher (ed.), *The Age of Permanent Revolution: A Trotsky Anthology* (New York: Dell, 1964).

Westoby, Adam, *The Evolution of Communism* (Cambridge: Polity Press, 1989).

Wood, Ellen Meiksins, *Empire of Capital* (London and New York: Verso, 2003).

—— 'A Manifesto for Global Capital?', in Gopal Balakrishnan (ed.), *Debating Empire* (London and New York: Verso, 2003).

Index

INDEX